A CELEBRATION OF BEES
Helping Children Write Poetry

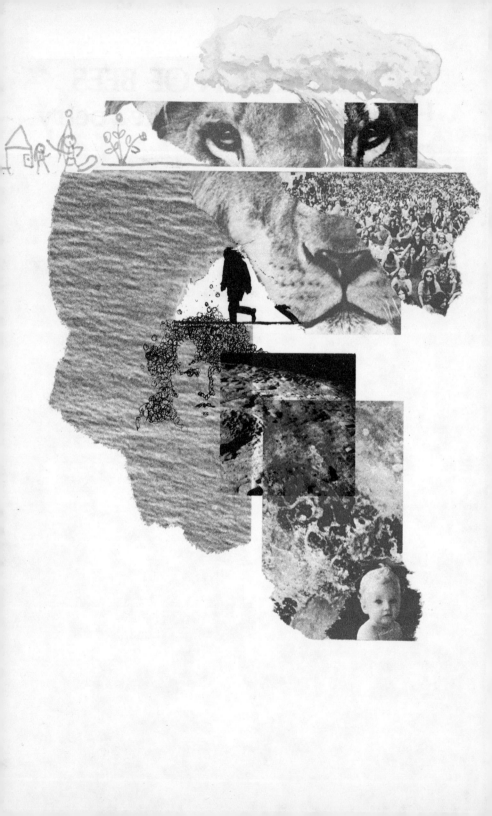

A CELEBRATION OF BEES
Helping Children Write Poetry

Barbara Juster Esbensen

Winston Press, Inc.
Minneapolis

Designer: Dick Martin

Copyright © 1975 by Winston Press, Inc.
Library of Congress Catalog Card Number: 74-24993
ISBN: 03-014401-9
Printed in the United States of America

Winston Press, Inc.
25 Groveland Terrace
Minneapolis, MN 55403

For my son
Peter Neil Esbensen
1951-1970
His dust is brighter
than all the air.

A Poet's Evaluation

The following evaluation of *A Celebration of Bees* was written by Ruth Whitman, a poet and teacher whose latest book is *The Passion of Lizzie Borden: New and Selected Poems.*

Books on how to teach children to write poetry tend to make me nervous. No matter how full of passion and enthusiasm the author may be, there is always the danger that teachers who read the book may believe that the instructions alone can serve them as a substitute for their own experience. But no one should attempt to teach reading and writing poetry without firsthand experience in *doing* both. This book could well serve as a guide to teachers who are willing to venture into those daring waters.

Barbara Esbensen clearly has the passion for poetry and the necessary experience in teaching and writing it. That she is an ingenious and enthusiastic teacher is demonstrated in her illustrations of how she has led children to observe aspects of their own experience, both external and internal, and to write about them.

Her book is easy to read, written in a chatty informal style, with chapters divided according to the ideas she has devised to stimulate children to write. Even the ideas that are familiar to poet/teachers are worth reviewing because Ms. Esbensen has an engaging way of presenting each lesson and offers new approaches, new examples, and a personal joy in their discovery.

Ruth Whitman
Author of five books of poetry;
teacher of poetry at the Radcliffe Institute;
co-founder and artistic director of
Poets Who Teach, Inc.

Foreword

For as long as I have known her, Barbara Juster Esbensen has had a love affair with words. And I have known her since she sat in my tenth grade English class, a small fourteen year old, judiciously alert and waiting for something wonderful to happen.

This air of optimistic expectancy has been characteristic of her all her life, but along with it was that rare ability to make things happen. In high school, involved in everything — the newspaper, art projects, plays — Barbara achieved her most spectacular triumph, it seems to me, when at the beginning of her junior year, she walked into the principal's office with a petition initiated by her and signed with fifteen hastily-scrawled names. It respectfully requested a course in "Creative Writing."

What words she found to answer the skeptically put "Why?" I never learned. They must have been effective though. She got her course, and while I know that the term "creative writing" is suspect today, remember that this was in a time when electives were few and a student's writing experience too often began and ended with the weekly theme.

How well I remember that oddly-assorted, earnest class. The bare room; the water-spotted window shades that never quite kept out the sun (nor did we want them to); the fun we had; the excitement generated; the small but daily satisfactions. How much we learned about each other and the world without and the world within. The other day I found one of Barbara's papers dating from that time. Her name in the upper right-hand corner and in the left "Just Scatterings" followed by: "Poetry is the wing tip of a thought." "Poems are tiny petals curled in the hollow of my heart."

I think what pleased me most, however, was the note affixed to the bottom of the page. In parentheses and followed by an over-sized exclamation mark was a big "(MORE IS COMING!)."

How much more neither of us could, at the moment, know, and that I suppose is the ultimate fascination of teaching.

In one way or another Barbara Juster Esbensen has been involved with the creative process all her adult life. As parent, artist, poet, teacher, she is convinced that given the proper stimulus all children — the gifted and the ordinary, though to her there are *no* ordinary children — are capable of breathtaking things in observing, in sensing mood, in seeing through to truth, and above all in finding language equal to their needs.

How a teacher can stimulate creativity in children is the substance of *A Celebration of Bees* and the astounding poems included in it, poems written by her students — children and young adults — are ample proof of the remarkable success of her method.

One of Barbara Esbensen's own poems, "Discovery," includes these lines:

> Split the shining ruby
> And find the star inside!

Helping to find "the star inside" is what *A Celebration of Bees* is all about. For children sitting right now in classes all over America waiting for something wonderful to happen and for those who merely wait, it could make *all* the difference.

Eulalie C. Beffel
English teacher, retired
East High School, Madison, Wisconsin

Table of Contents

Introduction   11
Words Are the Beginning   25
Sea Songs   35
Cinquain: Two, Four, Six, Eight, Two   47
Haiku   59
A Loop of Seasons   79
In All Kinds of Weather   99
City   117
Morning   133
Night and the Moon   143
People and More People   161
Animal Fair   183
Animating the Inanimate   197
Our Inner Spaces: Moods and Emotions   213
Now Let's Write About . . .   239
A Selected Bibliography of Poems for Children   255
Index of Poet's Ages   261

Introduction

"Is *swagger* a word? It is, ain't it, teacher?"

This is Susan. Her untidy red hair needs a barrette. As usual, tiny, mean points of light blaze in her defiant pale green eyes. Susan is ten, and she hates school. She hates the third grade with double intensity because she hated it last year, too. Susan hates reading books. She has not learned how to read well, and all books seem to exist just to trip her up. Her reading vocabulary on achievement tests is somewhere around first grade.

But she is asking about a word. A fine word: *swagger*.

"Yes," I tell her, "*swagger* is a word." Does she know what it means?

"Yeah, I know," she answers with a wild flipping of that lank, red skein. On her way back to her seat, down the long aisle of old desks bolted to the floor, Susan stops. She gives a boy one triumphant, hard whack on the head with the flat of her hand.

"Ha," she crows, "swagger *is too* a word and here it goes, right in my old poem!"

And then, with a final glower she adds, to the other thirty-four children, "and don't *nobody* else use it neither!" She flounces off to her seat. Nobody else uses it.

Later, when Susan, the nonreading, belligerent, school-hating Susan stands before the class to read her poem, this is what we hear:

Rain
"Rain swaggers across the street
Rain skips across the alleys
    of the world . . ."

In the third grade that year, thirty-five children from a "culturally deprived" neighborhood in a northern California city wrote their heads off. They wrote about everything and anything, as fast as ideas and images formed, with no concern about exact punctuation and perfect spelling. That would come later, with the polishing, with the writing of the thing beautifully on the coveted sixth grade paper, very white with no holes, and with bright blue lines. Their excitement, pride, and enthusiasm about writing carried into other subjects as well, perhaps because of the general atmosphere of successful personal achievement one could feel in the classroom. Writing became, for each of the children, a means to explore language, self, attitudes, and one's awareness of the world of real and imaginary things.

"Night," another nonreader told us in his poem, "is a black panther waiting to strike." Margie's parents had wanted to keep her in grade two another year because she seemed quite baffled by the printed word, and yet Margie could write an evocation of falling asleep, "the beds move in the night . . . ."

This book will set out for you the techniques I have found to be effective in generating enthusiastic responses to words and their creative uses. What I am trying to find with children and young people and what they and you, their teachers, must constantly look for are new ways to make our language express familiar experiences. We are looking for expression that is fresh, new, uniquely the writer's own.

Poetry as we use it here means language that excites. It means finding and using those surprising and just-right combinations of words that will delight us and astonish us with their newness.

Perhaps we forget something about our English language, since it is so commonplace a thing to us who speak it from birth. But it is interesting to know that English has been described by linguists to be one of the richest in the world. The writer Joseph Conrad was Polish. He spoke French, then learned English as an officer on English merchant ships. And when he began to write his great books, he said he never for an instant hesitated about the language he would use for his novels. He chose English for its tremendous variety, its shades of meaning, its richness, and its color.

It is this richness and variety that excites children and encourages them to play with words, to enjoy words for their sound, their color, and even for the shape of a particular word on the page.

As we look at what school children sometimes write as "poems," we can see that many teachers don't really know what real quality their students are capable of producing and that they have had no experience with ways to start young minds percolating with ideas. In these pages you will find hundreds of examples of poetry by children of all ages. And you will be able to see what sorts of questions one can ask young writers to consider, what kinds of probing and yet more probing must be pushed by the teacher before anything of value happens in the mind.

One June day when one of our children, George, was five years old, he rushed inside from the garden. Breathless, he dashed upstairs to find me.

"Mom!" he yelled. "Come quick! There's a celebration of bees out there."

Now *that's* poetry!

Later, when he was in second grade, he came home with a whole page of "poems" written by the class members.

"She says all the poems have to rhyme," he told me. And I read his "poem."

A Warm day
Is a May day
I lay in the hay
And hope to stay.

The rest of the efforts on the page — all titled "A Warm Day" — were nearly identical to his dismal collection of boring words. There was no attempt, obviously, to get those children to explore the idea of a warm day with their senses, with their lively children's minds, with enthusiasm. It's a far cry indeed from that jubilant "celebration of bees" shouted by a preschooler to the dull emptiness of day-hay-stay "poems" written for the second grade teacher. And I deplore the sad change in attitude toward language.

When people write creatively, they are actually seeing familiar objects or sensations or situations as though for the very first time. George said "a celebration of bees" because his uninhibited fresh mind felt that a swarm of bees, the sunlit garden, the sounds of early summer bird songs were a festive, lively, *celebration:* an accurate image. At three, Kai, another of our sons, excitedly told his father that the noisy fire in the big cabin fireplace was "roaring like a tiger" and that it was "waving like a flag." The huge blaze impressed him. He wanted to speak about it, so he compared it with two other things that immediately occurred to him. It is this spontaneous delight in words and self-expression that the techniques I've used throughout this book will help to encourage. I have found these techniques to be just about 100% effective, whether I've used them with seven or eight year olds, junior high school students, college people, or adults. They work equally well with people I meet regularly as a writing class and with children I've never seen before.

The poems you will read here were written by all sorts of children from every kind of background and degree of cultural stimulation. There are poems here by children from comfortable loving families, and by boys and girls from broken homes, from squalid surroundings and bitter parents. These children live in cities whose populations range from 30,000 to nearly 500,000 and represent both Seacoasts, the South, and the northern Midwest. The poems from Micronesia were written by young people, some of whom had never seen a city at all.

But, in the classroom, the magic of the written word becomes for all of them a means to add something to their lives and to soar above the commonplace, the trite, the used.

The book will show you one way of releasing the creative impulse that we all possess. Perhaps you have your own way of getting children interested in writing. There must be as many ways as there are teachers who love children's writing. If you do, there may be, even so, one or two ideas here that you can add to your own. If you have never tried to encourage children to write creatively, I hope this book will give you a way to begin.

What's in a Word

Emily Dickinson wrote in a letter once that if she should read something that made her feel "so cold no fire can warm me," and if the words made her feel as though "the top of my head were blown off," then she knew she was reading poetry.

When talking about poetry with children, I emphasize again and again that the poet wants to use our ordinary, everyday language in new ways; to make that language open new doors and windows for us; and to let us see old familiar things as though we'd never seen them before.

When he tried to see dirty, polluting smoke in some new way, Eric thought of as many words as he could. He wanted words that mean *dust, particle, grains, specks* — to describe what the smoke actually is. The surprising word he found in his mind, a word he didn't know he would find, was *spores*. It is exactly right and it is a new way for us as well as for Eric to look at smoke particles.

A frozen wind blows 'cross the town.
It flattens buildings and stirs up dust.
A harsh northwind blows spores of smoke
and it spreads and crinkles like papers
    on the street.
— Eric W., age 10

Any good descriptive writing can be "poetry" in this sense. Indeed, the book *A Stone, A Leaf, A Door* (Charles Scribner's Sons, 1948), edited by John S. Barnes, is the prose of Thomas Wolfe, culled from all of thousands of pages of his novels, set out on the page in short lines, and made brief enough so the impact of the words can hit us.

Writing poetry encourages children to be accurate, to say what they really mean, and to say it as economically as possible. No special language is necessary. No stylistic trimmings or tricks are necessary. What *is* necessary is to seek and find words that can capture the feelings and impressions we call experience, the all but inaudible music we sense in ourselves. To do this, we need not go down the June-moon-spittoon-baboon trail searching frantically for rhyming words. Poetry does not have to rhyme, or look a certain way on the page, or have lines that have a certain basic rhythm pattern. Today poetry is a capturing of essences, and words are the traps we set to do the job. Anything is fair game for the poet. There are no right subjects — and no wrong ones either. The poems you will find listed at the end of each chapter and those books of poetry in the bibliography at the end of the book will show you how diverse this world of poetry is for the contemporary reader.

In the pages to follow, you will meet the poems of Elvira M., a California third grader. When she came to my classroom, she was Spanish-speaking, with an incredible facility for the English language. For a solid year, Elvira wrote poems full of delicious images like this one from our "Rain" section.

When the raindrops fall
on a puddle,
They look like shooting-stars
in the blue mud-puddle sky.

In her "Wind" poem, she says the wind ". . . blows my hair / like purple thistles / in the sky . . . ."

When Elvira went into the fourth grade, we moved back to the Midwest, and she wrote to me fairly regularly for several years sending me her latest poems, which had undergone a sad change. One, written in fourth grade and called "The Butterfly," had these lines in it.

> The butterfly that went by
> To me once she said hi.

And the last, weary verse went:

> Right now she's in heaven,
> with 007.
> Where she will flitter and flutter
> With her wings as yellow as butter.

"Did you like them?" she asks at the end of her three-page letter full of similar work. "I think they're sort of . . . well I don't know. But I don't like them too much. Mrs. N. tells us poems have to rhyme."

From sixth grade, I received a letter from Elvira bearing the same edict: "I have not written any poems . . . because at my room Mrs. C. makes us write poems that rhyme and I cannot seem to make any that rhyme." Then she includes one "That I just wrote anyway. Not for Mrs. C.":

> The yellow and orange
> flowers
> are glittering
> in the sun.
> They want to go
> to London,
> to Paris,
> and
> New York.

I hope this has convinced you *never* to say "a poem *has* to rhyme." Generally speaking, I ask children not to use rhyme. It slows up the torrent of shapes, tastes, sounds, and colors that want to find places on their papers. Children will spend time lurching down the alphabet to find the rhyming words — and you'll end up with meaningless poems instead of the kinds of things children do best. Occasionally a poem "feels like rhyming." A few are included here, and those few somehow avoid the deadly sing-song characteristic of rhymes done by children.

I've lost track of Elvira over the years. One of the last letters I received from her when she was in the seventh grade asked me if I had saved "the poems I wrote when I was in third grade." She asked me to send them to her. She was recalling some isolated single lines from memory and, obviously, contrasting them with the awful doggerel she was currently writing. I sent her poems to her, and I hope she still has them, for they have the unmistakable ring and flow of real poetry. When she was only a child, she was a creative writer. The stifling of that free-flying attitude toward words is unforgivable.

My hope is that this book will help you discover other Elviras among the children you teach.

Some Ways To Use This Book

Each of the chapters deals with a particular subject you might want to use in introducing poetry writing to your students. They can be used in any order at all, except that I suggest you expose your young writers to cinquains before they tackle haiku, and those two chapters are arranged that way.

To get an overview of all the possibilities the book offers, you might want to read it straight through. On the other hand, if circumstances in your classroom, or in your part of the country, or your own preferences push you toward a particular subject or topic, start there.

The index of children's poems *by age of the child* can be helpful, I believe, when you want to let your own students hear what others who are their age have written. If you are new to this whole area of poetry writing by children and young people, the index by ages can afford you some insight into the capabilities of writers of a variety of ages.

I've included two kinds of bibliographies in the book. At the end of each chapter, you will find lists of individual poems written about the subjects covered in that chapter. At the end of the book are books of poetry whose quality and intent will show you and your children the diversity and beauty of contemporary (and almost contemporary) poetry. Some of these books are anthologies. Others are by a single poet. Some recordings and films are included as well.

It is essential that student work be reproduced from time to time for everyone to read. Just typing one example, at least, from *each* young writer and making ditto copies for everyone will give the new poets the satisfaction of seeing their work in print with a by-line. Occasionally, I've had a student who wanted to remain anonymous, or who used initials only, or a pen name. Fair enough. The important thing is to get the pieces printed.

Although spelling and punctuation are not our concern when we're in the white heat of writing images and ideas on paper, it is important to attend to some of the mechanics of writing when the poem is formed at last. I like to ask students to give me a copy of their work and to keep a dated copy for themselves.

This "finished copy" is the one the writers have checked to make sure words are spelled correctly and sentences are punctuated so they make sense to the reader. I emphasize that because the poem is now a completed fact, a creation, it deserves to be presented so it can be easily understood and appreciated.

It is from my collection of finished copy that I can select poems for reproducing. Sometimes with older students, my collection is turned over to a group of editors who do the selecting, always making certain that each student is represented by at least one piece. If you have done a good job of pushing young minds to think of "a better word, now a better one than that — now a stronger one than those two," there will be, in each child's work, something worthy of reprinting.

Enthusiasm for writing, a dawning realization that words are power, and a comfortable feeling about the whole business will pay off in many ways. We spoke of Susan at the beginning of this introduction. When Susan's poetry was printed, along with pieces by the other third graders, it turned out that Susan and the other non-readers could, indeed, read after all. They could read their own work and things written by the others. Slowly they began to get the idea about words. They began to have the glimmer of a feeling that words in books are after all just words "any old person" can put down for someone to read. Their active distrust of the snaky sentences and shifty punctuation on the printed pages of their books began to give way to this new understanding. Writing and reading are irrevocably linked.

And Now, Before I Say Anything

A college professor used to say, "Now, before I say anything this morning, I want to say something." Before I begin to talk about techniques that will help children to write, I, too, "want to say something."

If any one word can stand for the essence of creating a climate, an atmosphere that allows the creative impulse to grow and flourish, I think it would be the word *accepting*. Every child needs to feel that you respect and accept what he or she is trying to do. This does not imply dishonest praise for something that is not as good as it can be. It means that you exhibit an underlying understanding and respect for the children's efforts, while trying to bring out of those children the most exciting ideas they are capable of having.

It means that you can look for and find in their work something of real or potential value, something that can be talked about seriously with a view toward strengthening it, if necessary, of making it the child's own best effort.

Let me give you an example of some give and take between child and teacher.

> *Teacher:* Who has a good strong word to show how a cat moves?

Tim:	I wrote, "The cat moves slowly."
Teacher:	I can certainly see that cat as she goes so slowly along, Tim. I wonder if you could paint us a *clearer* word picture of what you are seeing in your mind. Let's see if there is a single word that means "move slowly," the way you want us to see your cat moving.
Tim:	How about *creeps?* The cat is moving slowly because it is after a bird. *Creeps* shows that, doesn't it?
Teacher:	*Creeps* is a good word. Can you tell me why it is even better than "moves slowly"?
Tim:	Because the word *creeps* lets you see the cat slung down along the ground after the bird. "Moves slowly" didn't show us how he looked at all.
Teacher:	Perhaps we can list even more words that are like *creeps.* Let's put them on the board for other children to use. . .

Every step of the way, the teacher shows acceptance, respect, and understanding for this child, even while the child is encouraged to *improve* the quality of his self-expression. Nowhere does the teacher say, "That's a dull way to write," or "You can certainly do better than *that,* Tim."

In a truly relaxed atmosphere, where only constructive criticism is offered by the children and by the teacher, any child will be able to develop real powers of written expression. There is, in this kind of classroom, no fear of ridicule, no agony of embarrassment, no sullen responses to repeated failure. No child will be unwilling to risk some far-out images, some grand experiments with the sound, color, texture, shape, or taste of language.

Can you maintain this climate? You must, or your efforts are doomed to fail. As a matter of fact, this is precisely the atmosphere one would hope for in *any* classroom, no matter what is being taught.

It has been my experience that this accepting classroom atmosphere, combined with the young poets' growing ease and familiarity with the world of words and frequent exposure to poetry by established writers will result in a new attitude toward literature. Having struggled with the medium themselves, the students become acutely aware of the frustrations and satisfactions all authors experience. Their appreciation of good writing develops because they know what the writer must go through to achieve it.

A boy from a "culturally deprived" neighborhood dashed to my desk one day with a poem he'd found by Emily Dickinson.

"She sweeps with many-colored brooms," he read. And then, with that feeling we all recognize when we've met something really fine, he added, "Jeez. I wish I'd thought of writing that."

Barbara J. Esbensen
Minneapolis, 1974

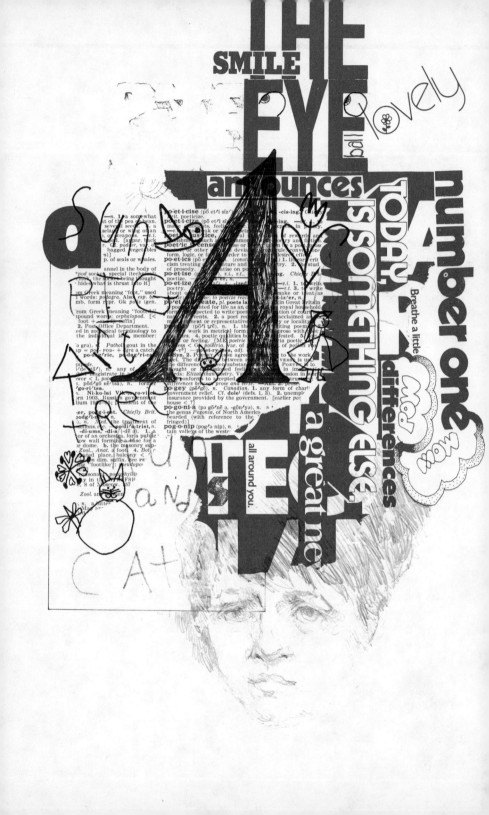

Words Are the Beginning

Words. All of our lives we live with words — spoken, written, read, heard. Words mold us, move us, stop us, start us. We seldom think much about them, and after years and years of using words, we have a tendency to employ them in pretty routine ways. Because a bland, colorless way of expressing ourselves can take over at a surprisingly early age, I believe it is essential that children be allowed to let their natural flair for imaginative thinking get a firm hold on their writing. Children should be encouraged to experience the work, the joy, the satisfaction of having written something that's true, beautiful, and imaginative.

Sherwood Anderson once wrote in an essay that "one works with words and one would like words that have a taste on the lips, that have a perfume to the nostrils, rattling words one can throw into a box and shake, making a sharp, jingling sound . . . ."

This attitude toward language is one that we need to develop in ourselves and in the children we teach. Its playfulness suggests a comfortable relationship between the writer and the tools of writing. Its selectivity suggests the writer's never ending but highly interesting task of discovering exactly the right word for this feeling, that sound, a movement, a color.

So, let's begin by asking the children to find some words to "throw into a box and shake."

Start with *fire*. Fire has a feel. What is the feeling of fire? *Hot* is the word we all think of first. But other words mean hot, too. Do you know any? What words mean *fire*? What words mean *burn*? What other words tell us something about a fire? Do any flowers make you think of fire? Any tastes? Red chili peppers? What smells like fire? What animal moves like a flame? What bird? What is the opposite of fire? Do you like the names of jewels? Are any jewels like fire?

See fire. What is burning? How does it look? Can you hear the fire? It makes sounds that mean *hot* and *fire* and *burn*. What are some sound words for fire?

We need color now. What color is the fire? Can you see it there behind your eyes? Write down the fiery scenes you can see in your mind.

As the children think of words, write them all on the chalkboard where everyone can see them until there is a tapestry of potential images. As your own imagination suggests ideas to you, ask for more and more words. You may also want to suggest that the children write down the words that are on the chalkboard in case the words are erased before they are finished exploring for images.

Asking questions to draw out more and more vivid words works for very young writers, who are just beginning, and for older children and adults as well. There is something exciting and inspiring about a surface covered with potential poems. Your chalkboard should shimmer with its fabric of words, words, and more words!

One September in a small city in northern California, a group of third graders wrote their first mind pictures after a preliminary session of putting a barrage of words on the chalkboard. Here are some results that came out of the word shaking that day.

Crackle, crackle, t-t-t-t-t-. — David
Crackle, s,s,s,s,s,s, red hot, orange, red.
— John

A fire, crackle, blaze, help! — Neil
Red hot fire. People running and yelling
    and firetrucks coming. — Sharon
The flames grow bigger and bigger. They
    crack!
And crack! As they burn the
    trees. — Randy

George, a sixth grader, after fifteen minutes of thinking about fire, wrote the following poem.

Boiling
Steaming orange
The white wavers burn, scorch, crackle,
    roar, destroy, char,
and leave black singe.
— George, age 12

His vocabulary has grown since the days when he was eight years old. But he can write using the same idea starter — fire — that the eight year olds used.

Marilyn, an eighth grader, said that fire "charred and cindered all of the trees . . . ." The nice surprise in Marilyn's line is the word *cindered*, a verb not too often used!

Nouns used as verbs can do some lively things for us. Kelly, a fourteen year old, once wrote that the spring wind "daisied the meadows." You recognize that as a most accurate description. Our minds see those daisies being created by the wind blowing over the meadow.

Word exploration is exciting and rewarding in itself, whether an attempt is made to organize the words into recognizable poems or not. The images and sounds written on the board or on paper during a word shaking session form their own constellations of sound and color.

Here are the third graders again. Listen to their word playing with all sorts of topics.

Bells:

Bells ring with tinkle of color.   — Mike

Bong, tinkle, ding, dong, bang, red,
       gray, black, slow.   — John

Bong, bing, ding, dong, ring, cling, clang.   — Neil

On the seventh day the bells let out ringing
       noises. And you can hear the tinkle of the
       bells. And booming bells of the church.
    — Randy

Bells are everywhere. They are at houses on the
       doors of them. People ring them all the time,
       they glitter when they push it.   — Leanne

Hammers:

Kong, kong, bang, tonk, tonk.   — David

Gray and brown, sledge hammer, work
       hammer. It has this kind of noise —
       bank, clank.   — John

Hammer, ow! Bang, boom.   — Neil

A man hammering sounds like a crash on a
       board. And man hammering ling, ling,
       ling.   — Sharon

Hammers will boom and crash. They will clink
       and clank. They are very clinking sounds.
    — Leanne

Wind:

The wind blow. — Mike

Fast and slow. Someone is blowing air
out of someone's mouth. — John

Sway, swish, whooo. — Richard

Sail boats moving, kites flying. People
getting blown home. — Sharon

Steam Locomotive:

Ss, erk, boom. — Neil

Chug, chug, clang, black. — Richard

A train. Whenever it stops the steam
comes out. — Sharon

Rain:

The rain is color, sound.   — Mike
Pitter, patter, splat, silver.   — Richard
The rain goes down like cats. The cats go down
    on an umbrella. It is a storm.   — Sharon

In the chapters that follow, you will read things
written by children of all ages. Keep in mind that before
young writers start a writing session, the same sort of
mental word stretching described above should go on.
Use it often for a surefire way to get the creative juices
bubbling. I can just about guarantee an explosion of ideas
and images on paper.

Explore different beginning words for poems. If
left to themselves, many people, children and adults as
well, will begin a piece of writing with *the*. Now there
is nothing wrong with *the* — it is a useful and necessary
word. But it gives the effect, sometimes, of a heavy,
dull, clumpiness that can slow down an otherwise lively
poem. So, every once in a while, it is a good idea to
remind children — and ourselves — that the language
is crammed with millions of words, none of them being
the, all waiting for a chance to become the first word
of a poem! Make a rule now and then, to be respected
as rules for writing haiku and cinquain are respected:
for one week no poem will allow itself to begin with
the.

This rule might cause consternation at first. As you
will see later in the book, a whole classroom of third
graders once began their poems about the sun with "The
Sun. . . ." "The Sea . . ." appeared on many papers too.
It is not a crime to start a poem with *the*. But, as
children become more and more aware of the thrilling
possibilities of language, they will find more vigorous
ways to begin their poems.

A poem can begin with a questioning word.
Who. . .? What. . .? When. . .? Why. . .? Did. . .?
How. . .? If. . . then. . .? Words like *when* and *where* can

be used not only to ask questions but also to make statements: "When it rains. . ."; "Where lilies grow. . ."; "When time isn't clocked . . . ."

A poem might also begin with a word ending with -*ing*. Have the class create a poem together. Pick a topic; any one will do. A season, a time of day, a building, a portrait, an animal. Suggest that every first line start with an -*ing* ending word. How might you use words like *flying, riding, leaping, sliding, growing, inching, crawling*? Write all the words on the chalkboard. Then collaborate; see what you can say about your subject with strong, lively -*ing* words.

Try the same kind of class collaboration using words that end in -*ed. Blended, marked, blackened, pillowed, pointed, started* might all be good words to start a poem about fire, smoke, or some other topic.

What adverbs can the children think of? Suggest they start poems with some -*ly* adverbs: *lightly, sprightly, slowly, newly, brokenly, raggedly.* Or they can invent words as Kelly does in her poem in the "Morning" section of this book. She used the word *sunly;* then she made up another word, *lemoned,* using it as a verb to tell us what the "morning sunly" did.

A poem's mood can be made more immediate and personal if the pronoun *I* or *you* or *my* is used. Sometimes specific names of people, places, flowers, animals make a poem more interesting and more immediate.

Once you've introduced your class to these different ways of beginning poems and have collaborated on one or two poems, you can write first lines on the board. If some children are excited about the possibility of using one or more of the lines in a poem of their own, that's perfectly fine. Those lines can then become the exclusive property of the children who choose them. Or the whole boardful can be fair game for all. In fact, it is often interesting to see in how many different directions a poem can go, given an identical first line. Either way is fine. Try them both.

Open up one of the books of poetry suggested in the bibliography at the end of this book and look at the ways in which its poems start. Read some first lines aloud to the children to see how they respond. Ask the children if they would have chosen the same first word. Why? Why not? What would be another choice for the first word? Another, another? Can they tell from the first line what the rest of the poem is going to be like?

If you begin this exploration of their language with the children, you'll find a comfortable relationship growing between them and their ability to handle the written word. Their attitude toward other poets — whether famous, published, or classmates — will develop into one of understanding and respect. They will begin to identify with the thought processes that take place inside a writer's head before a poem is written. Like the eight year old mentioned in the introduction, children will have a heartfelt appreciation of good writing, often accompanied by the fervent, "I wish I'd thought of writing that."

And when their own writing falls short in their own eyes, it will be because they have set some standards for themselves, based not on what the teacher likes, but on what they've come to recognize as effective, clear, and inventive use of language. This is what poetry is all about.

This book has two aims. First, it seeks to help you, to *urge* you to present children with endless opportunities for exploring their own language and for exploring ways that they can use that language to express their own ideas. Second, this book seeks to make you, the teacher, an appreciator of the lively things children can do with words. If these aims are fulfilled, your students will become both users and appreciators of the process writers everywhere have always employed in order to create life from words.

In this book we will look at writing about many different topics: people, animals, weather, oceans, the time of day. Of course, all of these topics and exercises could be used for stories as well as for poems. But story writing is another subject entirely and deserves a book of its own. The children's work reproduced in this book and the work your children produce from the ideas in this book will take the form of poetry, few words instead of many. (Some of the chapters contain a few passages of short poetic prose dealing with the subject. These, too, demonstrate how children can creatively handle language. "In All Kinds of Weather" contains short prose weather myths written by third graders in conjunction with a science project.) And those words will be a delight to our senses and to our sense of what writing creatively is all about.

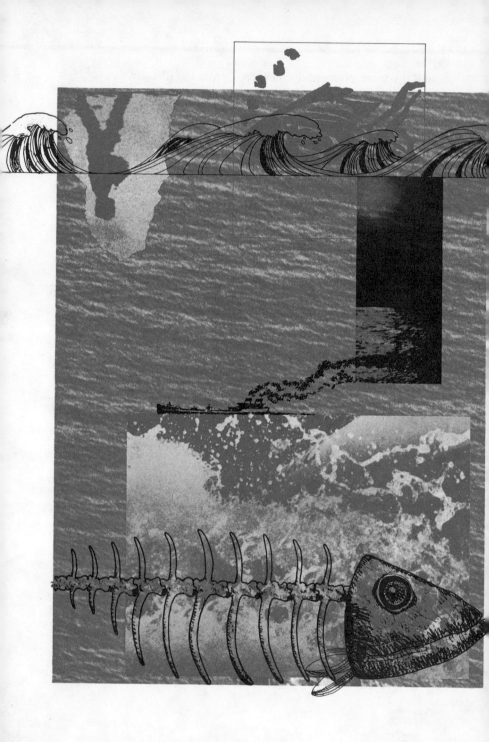

Sea Songs

Probably nothing in nature has been used quite so frequently as the sea for subject matter in poetry and prose. For those who live near the ocean, its moods, its sounds, its smells, and the creatures and plants beneath and around it all become part of their lives. For inland dwellers, the sea can be a far-off mystery to be deliciously imagined, vicariously enjoyed. All of the poems in this chapter, with one exception, were written by children in northwestern California or by Micronesian young people from the scattered islands in the western Pacific which form the U.N. Trust Territory.

The Micronesian students spoke and wrote English as a foreign language, so their problems of self-expression were similar to those of native English speakers eight or nine years old. We worked together in the same way I worked with other students. We began by filling a chalkboard with words and images. Then we spun off into associations that resulted from continual pulling out of words and questioning their meanings.

Begin with the sounds of the sea. Think about the way waves move toward the shore. See how they build and build into a long curve. See and hear that curve curl over and strike the land. Are the waves strong? Are they heavy? What sound does that great volume of water make when it reaches the shore? What word conveys that sound? What else makes such a noise?

Here are some third graders' impressions of the sounds made by waves.

The sea roars.
It is silver,
and it reflects
on ocean liners.

— Chris, age 8

When thunder comes,
the sea sounds
like roaring tigers.
It races to shore
and races back.
It looks like
green, blue, and white
flowers.

— Delayne, age 8

"There are many noises in the sea," eight-year-old Diana wrote, and she added:

The sea roars like lions
all through the day.

Another child hears a different kind of sound at the sea's edge.

Sounds of the sea gulls
lead the way
to the sea —

— Marlene, age 10

Listen to the almost deafening sound as Irene repeats *roaring* in her poem.

> The sea is sometimes fearful
> and sometimes gentle.
> But the sea sometimes has visitors
> that come to join the roaring party
> of the sea.
> They are dressed in rainbow colors.
> And the roaring breakers
> come breaking up
> the roaring party.
>
> — Irene, age 9

The main images of these poems convey the sea through its sounds. They contain words that sound like the sounds the sea makes.

Poets often use the sounds within words to convey a particular image. Say these words aloud and listen to the sounds they make: *crack, splat, smack, glitter, break, slap.* The consonants *t*'s, *k*'s, hard *c*'s make these words sound harsh. The short vowel sounds, in all but *break,* help evoke a feeling of quick motion. They can speed up the action of a poem and sometimes harden it.

But there are other words that we naturally linger over: *roll, roar, pound, smash, boom.* Long vowel sounds, combination sounds like *ou,* and softer consonants, especially the *sh* sound, contribute to a feeling of slowness. These words can slow down the action of a poem and make us aware of bigness, lengthiness, power. Compare the sounds in "heavy boulders" with the sounds in "little pebbles." See how much more quickly the words "little pebbles" move.

In this next poem, Neil uses drawn out words like *booming, crashes,* and *looms* to suggest a feeling of bigness and power. Notice how he takes his time before he lets you see that his word portrait of the sea is a night scene.

The sea is like a booming drum.
It crashes the salt water
against the reflection of the light
from the lighthouse
that looms
against the cliffs
and guides the ships
home.

— Neil, age 8

After a morning of experimenting with the effect sounds have on the pace of a poem, Linda wrote the following poem to show a quiet scene and a smooth night sea.

The sea is soft at night,
and shines
like gold.
The moon shines
like a silver dish.

— Linda, age 9

Read the poem aloud. It is almost impossible to rush this poem. We seem to want to stay with words like *soft, night, shines, gold, moon, silver.* Linda has achieved the effect she wishes by her choice of words and by the way those words sound. Creating word images depends on listening with the inner ear as well as seeing with the mind's eye.

> The sea's bouncing.
> It jumps and storms and falls —
> The waves look white as paper
> and it sucks the sands from the shore.
> And the sea
> is mighty terrific!
> — Tom, age 9

The most startling image in this poem is the "sea's bouncing." *Bouncing* is a good example of the kind of unusual and descriptive movement word that can come from the word shaking sessions at the chalkboard.

David sees the ocean in two moods.

> The sea is like a hill
> when it goes up and down.
> The sea is like a volcano
> that roars.
> The sea is like a cup of water
> if you push it up and down.
> The sea has two lives —
> One roars, and the other
> is smooth.
> — David, age 9

A Micronesian student also writes of the opposite moods of the familiar sea. She personifies the sea and the wind as they meet each other.

He is full of wonders . . .
He is so strange that he can lift
The biggest ship ever built,
But he can't lift the smallest stone
Ever found.
He is at peace only
When the wind
Is being easy on him.

When Wind comes along
Struggling and blowing hard,
He, too, struggles hard,
Making lots of noises.

When Wind sympathetically draws himself
Somewhere in a corner
of the skies,
He becomes so glassily smooth
that I, a curious girl,
Wish to walk in high-heeled shoes
on his surface
And watch the wondrous lives
beneath me.

— Maria R., age 17

Notice how the word *struggle* shows the interaction between the sea and the wind. And then suddenly we see the struggle end; we see an absolutely calm, unmoving surface. The surface is "glassily smooth," calm and steady enough to be walked on "in high-heeled shoes."

The incongruity of the sea being able to lift the "biggest ship ever built" but unable to lift the "smallest stone ever found" tells us something about the physical properties of the sea. It's the common physical phenomenon, water displacement, which we have all puzzled over, stated in a wonderfully fresh way. These images are what makes this poem work so well.

David spoke of the sea as "a hill." In this next poem, Masaharu, a Micronesian student, uses that same image. He repeats the phrase "rolling hills of waves" and the words *foam* and *roll* to achieve the feeling of the forward and backward, onrush and retreat, motion of endless waves.

When your rolling hills of waves break
on the reef, tops are concealed by snow.
Yet, what I see is not snow, but foam,
and the foam I see is no longer foam,
but again,
the rolling hills of waves.

When the dancing waves roll and roll,
crushed and broken by the reef,
I shall hear your calls in rhythm.
But when I call for you,
You will not hear me,
for my voice shall drown
in the roaring music
of the dark blue sea.

— Masaharu, age 17

The Sea

The breakers
like a mountain range
put into motion,
like an angry beast.

Toward the isle,
white horses
swept ashore.

— Fabyan, early 20s

Jerry imagined a fish breaking through the water's surface.

The sea shines like crystals,
And when a fish jumps
Out of the water,
It breaks crystals,
One at a time.

— Jerry, age 8

Can you see those shiny crystals, harder and more fragile than you might expect water to be? Can you see them forming and breaking "one at a time"? Those last four words give a slow motion effect that prints, on our minds, the image of the fish's thrust, the water breaking apart, and the crystal beads breaking as we watch.

Colors come and go over the surface of the water, changing it from moment to moment, season to season. What makes the ocean's color? Let's name some of the colors we see in the sea. What makes the water blue? What is another word for blue? Another? Name other things that are blue. Can you compare the sea with these other blue things?

What about green? What else is green? Are there green gems? What are their names? Does a drop of green water have anything in common with a green gem? If you drop a big green jewel, it might break. What are some words that mean break? Can these words be used to describe water breaking against the shore?

What makes the ocean white? We saw in Tom's poem that "the waves look white as paper." Think of some other white things. Mike's poem needs some comparisons to make it more interesting. What could he have used to let us see those gray whitecaps more clearly?

The sea is blue when it is calm.
But, when it is stormy, it is white,
And gray whitecaps appear.

— Mike, age 8

Are there some pure white things in nature
that could be compared with the whitecaps on waves?
Is snow a good comparison? Why? Think of a kind of fabric
that is often white and may remind you of foam.
Can we see a lacy edge to a wave?

When is the sea gray? Can the sea be gray and
calm? If you imagine a calm, gray sea, can you compare
it with something else that is smooth and dull? Name
some gray things, metals, fabrics. Are there fabrics that
could be used to describe the mist, the fog, or the rain-
blurred skies above the sea? Can you compare the gray
sea with an animal? Stretch your mind and see things
you have not seen before.

Donna's poem is lively because of the carefully chosen words, especially the color image she uses.

> The sea is as green
> as cat's eyes!
> The waves are crashing
> against the rocks
> and the waves rock little fish
> and move things.
>> — Donna, age 8

The main technique I used was to draw out live, descriptive words about the ocean. You might also explore the feel of the water, the temperature, the salt, the sand. Or use any other aspect of the sea that strikes you or your students.

In her poem, Eva wants us to experience the coldness of the sea.

> The sea is as cold as a snowflake,
> Its shining waves go by;
> And when I think of a snowflake,
> I think of the sea, with a sigh.
>> — Eva, age 8

In another poem emphasizing the temperature of the water, Marcia repeats *cool* in order to let us feel this special quality of her sea.

> The ship in the cool sea,
> The fish in the cool sea,
> The water is a-splashing
> And a-dashing
> Against a thunder ship.
>> — Marcia, age 10

Water in general is a fascinating subject for poetry. If you feel too removed from the ocean, use a river, lake, puddle, or pond for subject matter. What do all bodies of water have in common? How are they different? You could go on and on, writing about water.

It occurred to me, when I had finished reading their sea poems to them, to ask the California eight and nine year olds how many had actually been to the beaches of the cold northern coast. To my astonishment, only a handful of children had seen the ocean. Yet through their imagination, perhaps with the aid of pictures they'd seen or facts they knew about the sea, they were able to evoke the ocean-ness, the sea flavor word pictures we accept as true in the best, the poetic, sense.

Bibliography

Lewis, Richard, ed. "The Sea." In *Miracles: Poems by Children of the English-Speaking World*, pp. 103-118. New York: Simon and Schuster, Inc., 1966.

Pratt, Agnes T. "The Sea Is Melancholy." In *The Whispering Wind: Poetry by Young American Indians*, edited by Terry Allen. Garden City, N.Y.: Doubleday & Company, Inc., 1972.

Sandburg, Carl. "Sea Wisdom," "Old Deep Sing-Song." In *Wind Song*. New York: Harcourt Brace Jovanovich, Inc., 1960.

Stoutenberg, Adrien. "Ocean." In *The Wind Is Round*, edited by Sara Hannum and John T. Chase. New York: Atheneum Publishers, 1970

Swenson, May. "The Even Sea." In *The Wind Is Round*, edited by Sara Hannum and John T. Chase. New York: Atheneum Publishers, 1970.

Teasdale, Sara. "Calm Morning at Sea." In *Collected Poems of Sara Teasdale*, edited by Marya Zaturenska. New York: The Macmillan Company, 1953.

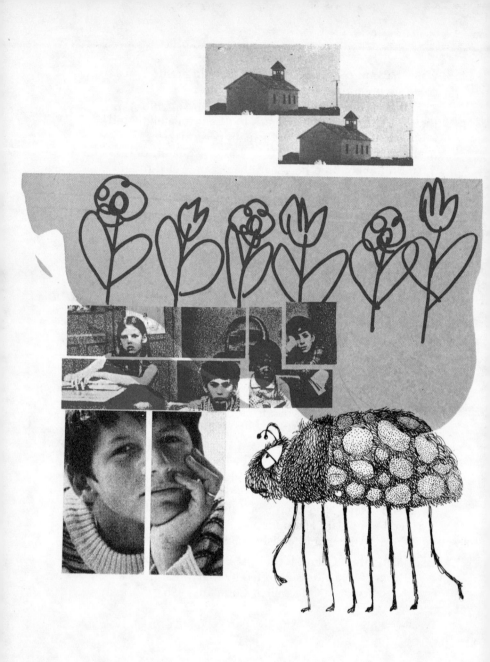

Cinquain: Two, Four, Six, Eight, Two

After early word experiments, I have sometimes found it to be a satisfying next step to work with the cinquain form. Cinquains were invented years ago by Adelaide Crapsey, an American poet who studied Japanese haiku.

Crapsey developed the form for a five line poem, in which the first line has two syllables, the second line has four, the third line has six, the fourth line has eight, and the fifth line ends the poem with two syllables. In her skilled poet's hands the cinquain became a subtle, sophisticated form.

Triad*

These be
Three silent things:
The falling snow . . . the hour
Before the dawn . . . the mouth of one
Just dead.

— Adelaide Crapsey

Writing in a form with a specified number of syllables demonstrates to students that much can be said in a few words. The syllable count forces writers to choose their words more carefully. A real mind stretching occurs as the poet searches for the right word with the right number of syllables.

The only caution I would offer at this point is that you urge your students to continue to search for just the right word. They should not fall into either cinquain

*From *Verse* by Adelaide Crapsey, Alfred A. Knopf, Inc., New York, 1938. Reprinted with permission of the publisher.

trap: choosing a word just because it has a certain number of syllables or adding inessential articles or adjectives to fill out the syllable count. The challenge in writing a cinquain is to find vivid words to express the writer's thoughts within the five line form.

Writing cinquains is a logical first step to writing haiku, a more complicated poetic form discussed in the next chapter. Haiku, with seventeen syllables, requires further comprehension of meaning and greater care in choosing words.

To introduce the cinquain, I first tell the children that we're going to write a poem together, that it will have five lines, and that each line will have a certain number of syllables in it. I tell them the name *cinquain* and explain its form. Then I show them the syllable count on the chalkboard like this:

$$2$$
$$4$$
$$6$$
$$8$$
$$2$$

I suggest that they write the numbers on a piece of paper. Then, as we work out a couple of cinquains using ideas from all the students, they write down the words for each line.

One afternoon I was invited to work with some sixth graders who had had little writing experience of the kind we've been discussing. After talking about the power of words, we decided to think about the idea of a storm. First we filled the chalkboard with storm words. What does a storm look like? What color is it? What does it sound like? What instrument in the orchestra sounds like a storm? What does a storm smell like? What does the air feel like right before and after a storm? We filled the chalkboard with words and I introduced the cinquain. The children decided on the two-syllable word *thunder* for the first word.

Now the cinquain-to-be on the chalkboard looked like this:

2 Thunder
4
6
8
2

What should the four-syllable line say? "Lightning flashes" was the unanimous choice, and the cinquain continued:

2 Thunder
4 Lightning flashes
6
8
2

Now for a six-syllable line, I encourage, warning about careful syllable counting. One of the girls suggested a line. We can see how the poem developed:

2 Thunder
4 Lightning flashes
6 Jagged streaks, cymbal strikes
8
2

The word *cymbal* was one of the chalkboard words suggested in response to the question, "What instrument of the orchestra reminds you of a storm?"

The eight-syllable line seems incredibly long to children; it has acres of room compared to the two-syllable first line. See how this fourth line rolls along:

2 Thunder
4 Lightning flashes
6 Jagged streaks, cymbal strikes
8 Howling organ — wind bellowing
2

And now we are at the end, in need of a two-syllable line that will clinch the poem. This last line can have an interesting effect on the reader. It brings a finality to the poem in one of several ways. The two beats can sound hollow, like the voice of doom, the end. Adelaide Crapsey's line, "Just dead," gives that feeling. Or they can be a frantic cry or a neat summing up; or they can be humorous, as we'll see in some of the cinquains in this chapter.

Following some lively debate and deliberation, we finally agreed that our joint-effort poem would look like this:

2 Thunder!
4 Lightning flashes —
6 Jagged streaks, cymbal strikes,
8 Howling organ — wind bellowing.
2 Help me!

We added punctuation marks to make the poem clearer. This completed our cinquain, a strong statement about a storm.

Writing one or more cinquains as a group seems to motivate individual effort. As children begin their own cinquains, remind them that the number at the beginning of each line is there to indicate how many syllables they should have in that line.

In order to help the children answer the what-shall-I-write-about question, I like to have a mystery box ready, filled with slips of folded paper, each containing an idea for a poem. These poem starters can be nouns, subjects for poems, words they might use in the poem, action verbs that might suggest a poem, anything that might set their imaginations on fire.

Each child reaches into the box and chooses his or her own slip. I am careful to point out that this slip of paper is a thought starter only. If children have their own ideas, they are free to use them.

Before the children begin writing, review some of the exciting words that can begin a poem: the question words, *who, what, why, where, when;* the action words; and the *-ing* words. Encourage the students to brainstorm for themselves, using their idea starters, to think of colors, shapes, smells, in the same way they would search as a class for words to fill the chalkboard on a given topic.

In the following poems, the title is usually the starter word or idea from the mystery box.

Earth
The earth,
Planet of life,
A Planet of beauty;
Planet in the dark void of space:
The earth.

— Douglass, age 11

Spider Web
Morning,
Glistening in sun,
Cool breezes blow on webs,
Fly trapped in the colors of it,
No more.

— Elizabeth, age 11

51 *Cinquain: Two, Four, Six, Eight, Two*

Spider Web
Knitting,
Weaving, testing,
Calculating. Feeling
her trap to tangle victims in:
Deadly.

— George, age 12

The Storm
Thunder!
Lightning flashing!
Black moonless, starless sky;
Thunder rolling like a bass drum.
The storm.

— Stanley, age 11

Stanley's mystery slip contained the same topic the
class had chosen for its poem. However, even though
he uses some of the same words, notice how he
focuses on different sights and sounds.

The people in the writers' lives make good
subjects for cinquains.

My Brother
Tony,
My dumb brother.
Inconsiderate, too;
Menace of Atlanta, Georgia:
Brother!

— Stanley, age 11

Stanley told us that the final word was pronounced
bro-*ther*, giving his cinquain a humorous twist.

All sorts of people can be inspiration for cinquains
(and other poems). So put some names in your mystery

box; use real people, folk heroes, and silly strange names that make the writers want to describe the person who owns that name.

Historical figures, real or legendary, as well as people in the writers' lives make good subjects for cinquains.

Paul Revere
He rode
To warn people
That the Britishers came
To rob, kill, and squash the people.
He rode.
— Ruthie, age 10

Charles de Gaulle
Big nose,
Talks with a roar,
Six feet five, quite alive,
Perfect image of Frankenstein.
Bye, France!
— Ellen, age 11

Matt Dillon
Dillon,
Tall as the West,
Marshall of Dodge City,
Keeper of law and order —
Big man.
— Philip, age 11

In a poem we are always looking for fresh language, a new way to say something. Philip's image of Matt Dillon as "Tall as the West" is a good one.

When Mike picked "Jack and Jill" from the mystery box, neither he nor the class expected the poem that resulted.

53   *Cinquain: Two, Four, Six, Eight, Two*

Jack and Jill

Water,
Well on a hill.
A gay group of children
Sliding down a hill, thinking death —
Poor kids!

— Mike, age 11

The circus has an endless supply of poem starters just waiting to be used. Put some circus ideas on slips of paper in your mystery box. They never fail.

The Clown

Funny —
He makes me laugh,
Waddling Mr. Clown
When you ride in a ring car,
HA HA!

— Tina, age 12

The three action words, *soaring, swooping,* and *catching,* combined with the long vowel sounds in the poem give us a very distinct picture of the majestic eagle.

Animating the inanimate is still another way to make an ordinary idea come to life, a fresh way of stating something we all may have thought about.

Morning

Morning
Comes on the night
like a robber stealing
something precious from a big house.
Morning.

— Ellen, age 11

This image catches our attention, for not only does it personify morning, it also reverses the way poets have often depicted morning and evening. Evening in poems has been referred to as stealing the light or stealing away the day. But, here, morning is compared to a thief, stealing the dark jewels of night.

This quiet scene is not an animation, but a picture of an animal at night.

Swan
Moonlight
A swan is still,
He lifts his graceful head
And slowly descends in the light . . .
Gone now.

— Tina, age 12

Tightrope Walker
Brave man
On a high wire
Above the spellbound crowd.
Like a spider on its silk web,
He glides.

— Joseph, age 13

Cinquains which begin with *-ing* words can present powerful pictures. In the following poem, Bert uses strong, dramatic words.

Race
Screeching!
Crash violently
Cars burn. Rubber! Smash! BAM
Car explodes violently — AAH
But wait . . .

— Bert, age 11

This is a good example of the surprise ending, the twist the last line can give a cinquain. What really happened? Was there a crash? Why wait?

A good *-ing* word starts us off with the feeling of flight in this next poem.

Eagle
Soaring,
Swooping down from
High on the mountain tops,
Catching animals from the air.
Eagles.

— Dave, age 11

By this time it must be obvious that ideas for cinquains, like ideas for any other kind of imaginative writing, exist everywhere. One is limited only by the number of lines and the syllable count. Stretch your minds and imaginations with words, and the form and syllable counting will only make your expressions more interesting.

Turn your students loose with 2 — 4 — 6 — 8 —2. Good things will happen. And on to haiku.

Bibliography

Crapsey, Adelaide. *Verse*. New York: Alfred A. Knopf, Inc., 1938.

Hopkins, Lee B. *City Talk*. New York: Alfred A. Knopf, Inc., 1970.

Haiku

What Is Haiku?

After children have become accustomed to the restrictions of cinquain and to its delightful possibilities, they can tackle the even more restrictive haiku form.

Haiku is a Japanese form of poetry that calls for seventeen syllables in three lines. The lines have syllable counts of five, seven, and five. Three other general rules must also be followed if the writer's end result is to be a genuine haiku.

First, a haiku must *refer in some way to nature.* The poem doesn't have to be about nature; but there must be a nature clue or reference included in it.

The second requirement for writing haiku is that the poem should *refer to a particular event as it is presently taking place.* The haiku writer must focus on a specific occurrence. (A robin eating a worm is an immediate, specific occurrence; the return of spring is not.) Nor can the specific event be described in the past tense. Haiku uses only *now* words!

Using a particular event is essential to writing haiku according to Harold G. Henderson in his excellent book *Haiku in English.* "The idea is so fundamental in Japanese haiku," says Henderson, "that we do not believe any poet attempting to write haiku in English can ignore it and still write haiku." Generalizations do not belong in haiku.

Rule three requires that the haiku *suggest to the reader the emotions the poet feels* while describing the particular event.

Although some practitioners of haiku in English don't feel bound by these rules, I find that most people — and especially beginners — do their best work in this strict form. Like the writer of haiku in Japanese, the English-speaking haiku poet must cope with the limitations imposed by the seventeen syllables. The poet's words must therefore be carefully chosen, and the poetic idea must be focused and distilled into a clear expression of the original thought. The experience is valuable for any writer at any age.

In this chapter, we will be talking about haiku in which the poet objectively *observes* a relationship between separate things. Even though the poet hints at or expresses an emotion about what is being observed, he or she is essentially an outside observer, not a part of what is being observed. Haiku that depends on visual impressions is sometimes called picture haiku. The challenge is to make these delicate pictures as clear as one can, using only the seventeen syllables.

Look at the comparisons in this poem by Bashō, a Japanese writer (1644-1694).* In the original Japanese, this haiku followed the 5-7-5 format, but Henderson, the translator, has chosen not to follow that form in his rendition.

On a withered branch
a crow has settled —
autumn nightfall.

Can you see the withered branch, night coming, and the small crow silhouetted against the autumn sky? Is there a suggestion of the poet's emotions in this poem? What might they be?

Objective haiku also makes use of other senses

*From *An Introduction to Haiku* by Harold G. Henderson. Copyright © 1968 by Harold G. Henderson. Used by permission of Doubleday & Company, Inc.

besides sight. Here is a poem by Anne Rutherford from the book *Borrowed Water: A Book of American Haiku.***

> South-bound roaring past
> splintering the night with sound —
> listen! a cricket.

To show us a night scene, the poet compares two sounds. Do you hear the train shattering the night? Do you then hear the soft, nightsound of the cricket? In the following poem, a combination of two senses is used.

> Reddish rhubarb stems
> sprout among patches of snow
> In the cool spring air.
> — Leslie M., age 11

This poem shows us an early spring scene with rhubarb leaves just beginning to sprout and patches of snow on the ground. We see the leaves and the snow; we feel the cool air.

Leslie wrote this poem, too.

> When the warm sun shines,
> Little buds shoot up among
> Whitened, stiff cornstalks.

Is it haiku? Ask yourself, "Does it describe a *particular* event, or is it a description of something that happens generally in spring? Unlike Leslie's first poem, this one is a generalization and therefore not strictly haiku.

Perhaps you can rewrite it to make it a description of a particular event. How could this be done? "Whitened stiff cornstalks" does have the clarity of an event seen *now*. Maybe what is needed is a more definite picture in

---

**From *Borrowed Water: A Book of American Haiku* by the Los Altos Writers Roundtable, Charles V. Tuttle, Co., Rutland, Vt., 1966, page 79. Reprinted with permission of the publisher.

lines one and two. We need to experience what is happening *here* and at *this* moment. Would naming the kind of "little buds" help? Try some variations and see for yourself.

How to Begin

We have already placed much emphasis on word play as a way to begin writing poems. Word play is important in writing any poem. But in a strict form such as haiku and cinquain, in which the writer is limited to a certain number of syllables and the right word must be found, word play can be even more beneficial.

I've found that a good way to help children start writing haiku is to have a few class sessions with ideas going up on the chalkboard and all the children contributing to the work at hand.

To begin, I put a five-syllable first line on the chalkboard and ask the children to compose the second and third lines. This generates interest immediately. Everyone can contribute to the poem and can have a chance to try something new without the frustration of having to work the whole poem out alone.

Take a look at this five-syllable first line.

Feet squeaking on snow.

I wrote this haiku line on the board and asked the children to complete it, keeping in mind the following requirements: let us know somehow that it is almost dark outside and that the poet, while walking along, is either thinking about or actually seeing supper being prepared. I find that setting certain requirements like these sharpens the students' awareness of what words can do.

A different set of requirements to go with the same first line could have been: in lines two and three, let us know that it is a clear, cold, sunlit day in January and that the poet, while walking toward the skating rink, is aware of sharp blue shadows on snow.

If you will stop right this minute and try writing two haiku with the different sets of requirements in mind, you will see how different the word pictures will be.

After the children have suggested lines for the group haiku, I ask them to write a poem individually. Here are some haiku that resulted from the original first line.

Feet squeaking on snow.
  Breathing in all the night air
    The scent of supper.
                      — Jennifer B., age 13

Feet squeaking on snow.
  When lights begin to shine bright —
    Hot, steaming supper.
                      — Tina, age 12

Feet squeaking on snow.
  The street lights have just flicked on —
    Clattering of spoons.
                      — Rita, age 10

Rita had a terrible time trying to get the clue about supper into her poem. I think you'll agree that her solution is a marvelous one. The two fine words *flicked* and *clattering* show that earlier practice with word play certainly paid off for Rita.

Debbie found herself with two poems.

Feet squeaking on snow.
  Just can't wait for supper — mmm —
    Shadow by moonlight.

This is her second poem.

Feet squeaking on snow.
  The strong night wind pushing you —
    toward the scent of food.
                      — Debbie, age 13

When Debbie read these aloud, the children felt that
neither was quite right. Line two in the first poem sounded
"blah" to them; line three in the second poem seemed
"boring for a haiku." After some hotly debated suggestions, Debbie came up with the obvious answer.

> Feet squeaking on snow.
> The strong night wind pushing you . . .
> Shadow by moonlight.

She sacrificed the supper clue, but combined the best
of the two poems to come up with a poem which pleased
everyone.

Joseph reported that he had "messed around"
with my suggested first line and just couldn't come up
with a poem he liked. So he wrote his own first line
and the following poem.

> The dim winter light —
> Peering through steaming windows
> With hot food ready.
> — Joseph, age 13

Joseph didn't use the same first line as everyone else did, but obviously the line made him think about what he could put into a poem. He did fulfill the other requirements. He explained that the dash after *light* indicates a "sort of stop" and that someone is inside peering out through a steaming window. Joseph felt that no punctuation at the end of the first line would make us think the winter light was doing the peering. What do you think?

I had some fourteen-year-old students suggest some first lines. They came up with these:

The pond is stagnant
Winter's proudest crown
Reflections in glass
Children in the rain

And here are some of the poems that these first lines suggested.

Winter's proudest crown
   Birch trees dotting the landscape
    With a rust mantle.
          — Chris, age 14

Reflections in glass —
   Sunrise flowing into it
    And silence throughout.
          — Caroline, age 14

Children in the rain —
   The sound of many horses?
    It's only small Jill . . .
          — Caroline, age 14

Of the three, "Children in the rain — " is the best haiku. It shows us something about the weather. We know that the poet, hearing a lot of noise, is surprised that only one child is making the noise.

Could the other poems be improved by working comparisons into them? Would using more specific words be any help? Try your hand at adding twelve syllables to each of the suggested first lines. See how well you do. You will be much more effective as a teacher of haiku if you've had the fun and frustration of tackling the form yourself.

A variation of the mystery box technique can be used for the first five-syllable lines of a haiku. Keep a box or jar filled with a supply of first lines, handy for the taking when children need them.

Since a haiku describes a particular event, you can also encourage the children to jot down notes on their own experiences and the things that happen around them. They should include details about plants, animals, and other things in their everyday lives. They can then go back to these notes when they need subject material.

There is another effective way to generate interest in writing haiku. In *An Introduction to Haiku,* Harold G. Henderson has given us his translations of original Japanese haiku. For each freely translated poem, he also presents the original haiku and his literal translation of each Japanese word.

I have found that it intrigues haiku writers to be given only this literal translation and to become the original writer of the haiku. I ask the student to try to get inside the mind of the Japanese writer who composed the poem so long ago and to write a haiku that will mirror the idea of the original writer. After the students write and read their poems, I put Henderson's professional one on the chalkboard so they can see how their work compares with his.

Here is an example of the way this works. First, the literal English translation from the Japanese is given to the children.

Sky | too | earth | too | are-not | only | snow
falls-ceaselessly

This is how some children expressed the thought of the writer.

> Snow keeps falling
> Everything has vanished now.
> Where did it all go?
> — Rita, age 10

> Ice encrusts our house
> Neither sky nor earth are ours.
> Snow is our kingdom.
> — Ann V., age 14

> Earth has disappeared
> Only snow is there falling,
> falling ceaselessly.
> — Charlotte F., age 14

This example of literal Japanese intrigues children.

Snake | fleeing | me | had | looked-at | eyes'
grass-in remain

If one gets inside the original writer's mind, what does one find? What exactly did the long ago Japanese writer think about this particular snake? Where does the word *eyes* fit in? What does the poet want you to feel about the eyes? Think about this snake. How is it moving? Where is it? Does this interpretation say it as you might say it yourself?

> A snake looked at me —
> then fled, but the hostile eyes
> remained in the grass.
> — Lisa, age 14

Or this one?

> Warm summer night out.
> Snake slithers by the side-walk
> Eyes still watching me.
> — Debbie, age 13

Debbie's snake seems to live in the city.

Before you peek at the poems this next literal translation inspired, try writing a haiku yourself.

> Distant-mountains' | eye-jewels | in | reflect dragonfly

One group of children looked hard at a large color photograph of a dragonfly, noting its separate parts and its color. Then, remembering dragonflies each had seen in the long past summer, they wrote these poems. Rita added a color word to her picture.

> Aquamarine wings —
> the dragonfly's eyes reflect
> mountains far way.
> — Rita, age 10

And Jennifer imagined many dragonflies.

> Swarms of dragonflies
> their jewel eyes reflecting
> On the tall mountain.
> — Jennifer, age 13

As you can imagine, that word *on* in line three was loudly criticized. Jennifer countered with the argument that she needed five syllables and was stuck otherwise. Someone suggested that if she dropped the word *on* and settled for sixteen syllables, the poem would make sense. The children felt the sense of the haiku was more important than holding to seventeen syllables. To everyone's relief, Jennifer agreed.

Joseph had two variations, both of them delightful. Which do you prefer?

Pretty dragonfly,
  with jewels for eyes you fly
  and reflect mountains.

With jewel-like wings
  you fly with mirrors for eyes
  reflecting mountains.
                            — Joseph, age 13

This next literal translation was presented to a group of ninth grade girls whose ages ranged from thirteen to fifteen. Of all the Japanese poems, this one elicited the most enthusiastic response from them.

Spring-rain | grove | to | get-blown | thrown-away-letter

According to Henderson, "A Japanese letter would be written on a single long sheet of flexible paper." I mentioned this to the students and asked them to picture the rainy scene and to think of reasons why there might be a discarded letter in the grove. Without exception, the girls in the class all came to the same conclusion.

The ink weaves red paths
  I stand here in wet silence
  The letter is gone —
                            — Julie E., age 15

This next haiku sneaked by with six syllables in the last line. I included it here because of its wistful tone of resignation. Can you think of a way to change the last line to fit the format while retaining the tone of the poem?

> It was raining hard
>> When the wind blew his letter.
>> It often rains in spring . . .
>>> — Bonnie M., age 14

> Poor lonely letter —
>> All alone it bears the rain
>> Good-bye love. Good-bye.
>>> — Jacqueline, age 14

To those ninth graders, it was obviously a love letter. Henderson's version seems quite matter-of-fact in comparison.

Spring Rain
Rain on a spring day:
> to the grove is blown a letter
> someone threw away.

All of the following were written by ninth graders, using the literal translations that appear above them.

> Eleven-riders | faces | even | not-swing blown-snow

> Eleven riders'
>> Swarthy faces not even
>> swinging from blown snow.
>>> — Ann V., age 14

> Caged-bird | butterflies | envy | eye-expression

The caged yellow bird
  envies the spring butterflies'
  remorseless freedom.
                    — Kathryn, age 14

Poor lonely caged bird
  watches the free butterfly
  through the metal bars.
                    — Gail, age 14

High | noon | reed-sparrows | save-for | river's
sound | even | is-not

High noon brings calmness
  although reed sparrows still fly —
  Even the river sleeps.
                    — Charlotte, age 14

With high noon, the bird
  coming to the river's edge
  listens to the sound —
                    — Patti, age 14

Harold Henderson's book contains his translations
of over 300 haiku, with the original Japanese and the
English literal translation. I strongly urge you to buy
a copy. The book is a delight, and the literal translations
are a never ending challenge for haiku writers. Until

you do own your copy, use this additional list of literal translations.

> Winds | to | ask | which | first-ly | falling
> tree-leaf

> Butterflies' | lovingly-follow | flower-wreath
> coffin's | top

> People | go-home | afterward
> be-dark

> Moon | one-circle | stars | un-numbered | sky
> dark | green

> Short | night | shallows-in | remaining | moon
> one-part

Become a haiku writer by beginning with these starters. Then try them with your students.

Lead into Gold, Haiku's Alchemy

Why have we devoted so many pages to haiku? What can come from the writing of seventeen syllable, three-line verse? Why should you spend a lot of time getting your students to write in this specific form? Why introduce haiku at all? The answer becomes obvious if we examine the writing of children before and after they have worked with haiku.

Compare the two efforts that Tina made to describe playing in the snow. This is the first.

Playing all day —
Running and jumping in snow
Laughing all day
Even eating snow
But still having fun.

And this is the second.

Speeding down the hill
White soft snow higher than me.
Where are my mittens?
— Tina, age 14

In the first poem there is a loose generality of expression that seems bland and ordinary. In the haiku version, tautness and control are evident.

Here is another example. Joe, an eighth grader, was looking at an American history book, *This Fabulous Century* (Time-Life Books). He was especially taken with a section on old funny papers. The first thing he wrote expressed his feelings like this.

Me and my brother finally get the funnies. I grab
Flash to see if he kills the Monster and saves the
princess. But he's captured by the mad doctor
Zin and is held by a secret force that doctor
Zin invented. Shucks! Got to wait till tomorrow
to find out, doggonit.

When Joe used the same nostalgic pages for an idea starter to write haiku, here is what he wrote.

Way Back When
Wonder what happened
  To Flash Gordon and Tarzan —
    and Sunny Sundays.

— Joe, age 13

As you can see, this poem ignores two of the rules for haiku. It does not have a nature clue, nor does it describe something happening right now. However, its seventeen syllables crystallize Joe's thoughts. Joe commented that while writing the haiku he was aware for the first time of how un-funny the so-called funnies of the 1970s have become. The unexpected nostalgia of this thirteen year old came out in his haiku. And the other children in the group agreed that this haiku really said something to them. Jennifer felt it was "sad, but in a way I can't explain."

Over the years, I have found that haiku has a strong effect upon the writing of young people. Others have also found this to be true, as can be seen from this quote taken from *Borrowed Water: A Book of American Haiku.* ". . . The poets used the Japanese tone poem haiku to appreciate the syllabic content of words. Use of the haiku taught prose writers that brevity and simplicity improved their style."

Compressing and refining thought into seventeen syllables forces the writer to select precisely the words that suit the experience being conveyed. Students often say they chose a particularly apt word, one they wouldn't have thought of otherwise, because they needed a certain number of syllables. In their other writing, prose as well as poetry, students find a noticeable improvement after they have focused their minds on the restricted haiku form.

Films are an excellent way to generate creative electricity. (They can be used for any and all of the topics in this book.) One morning a group of freshmen girls watched the film *Goodnight Socrates* which concerns the trauma experienced by a long-established Greek community in Chicago when a freeway forces all of them out of their homes. Nearly all the film impressions handed to me that morning had the same conversational tone — a sort of bland reporting. No doubt I had not made myself clear when I asked for "lively, strong impressions," and the results were disappointing to all of us.

Yvonne's writing typifies that of the entire group.

I thought the movie was really good. It made one feel as if he/she were right there with the people. I thought I would cry when the man went to the tree behind the shop where he used to work. *Goodnight Socrates* was a good name for the show. The sounds were just right at the right time.

To achieve more power and clarity, we decided to rethink, in a haiku form, our reactions to the film. For this haiku there would be no special effort to speak about nature. Here are some seventeen-syllable poems that were the result of attempting to refine our thoughts about *Goodnight Socrates*.

As the building falls,
   I watch my life fall with it
      What is left for me?
            — Yvonne S., age 14

The fragile bubbles —
   Bright and gay as the sunshine . . .
      Where is her laughter?
            — Kristy K., age 14

It spins around me . . .
My last look at our small world . . .
Onward we must go.
— Roberta T., age 15

Only Forty days
until our little world dies.
Will we dance again?
— Jane F., age 14

Henderson tells us in *Haiku in English* that haiku writing teaches one how to recognize ". . . what is (or is not) important in any experience . . . ." He continues that haiku also teaches ". . . at least the beginnings of the art of compression. . . ." Certainly these are important lessons for anyone, child or adult, who wants to practice creative expression.

Bibliography

Atwood, Ann. *Haiku: The Mood of the Earth.* New York: Charles Scribner's Sons, 1971.

Bashō. *The Way of Silence: The Prose and Poetry of Bashō,* edited by Richard Lewis. New York: Dial Press, Inc., 1970.

Behn, Harry. *Cricket Songs: Japanese Haiku.* New York: Harcourt Brace Jovanovich, Inc., 1964.

Goodnight Socrates. Film, thirty-four minutes, black and white. Contemporary/McGraw-Hill Films.

Henderson, Harold G. *Haiku in English.* Rutland, Vt.: Charles E. Tuttle Co., 1967.

————. *An Introduction to Haiku.* Garden City, N. Y.: Doubleday & Company, Inc., Anchor Books, 1958.

Issa. *A Few Flies and I: Haiku by Issa,* edited by Jean Merrill and Ronni Solbert. New York: Pantheon Books, Inc., 1969.

Lewis, Richard, ed. *Of This World: A Poet's Life in Poetry.* New York: Dial Press, Inc., 1968. (Author's note: The Japanese poet, Issa, is one of the most famous Haiku poets.)

Los Altos Writers Roundtable. *Borrowed Water: A Book of American Haiku.* Rutland, Vt.: Charles E. Tuttle Co., 1966.

Moore, Lilian. *I Thought I Heard the City.* New York: Atheneum Publishers, 1969.

Stewart, Harold. *A Chime of Windbells: A Year of Japanese Haiku in English Verse.* Rutland, Vt.: Charles E. Tuttle Co., 1969.

A Loop of Seasons

Summer, fall, winter, spring. The seasons of the year affect what we do, what we eat, how we feel. And they are great subjects for poetry.

Poets have traditionally celebrated all the seasons from their own perspective, their own time. From the Romantics, who felt close to the growing season, close to the earth, we have odes to autumn, commemorating the harvest. Haiku writers, as we have seen in the last chapter, often express a perception of the season of the year in writing about specific natural events.

Contemporary poets, children or adults, can write about the seasons from their own perspective. Whether they live in an urban, suburban, or rural area, in a temperate climate or a seasonal one, people can heighten their powers of perception and creative expression by watching and writing about the seasons.

Who doesn't know the feeling of spring fever, winter doldrums, summer lazies? Who hasn't been inspired and exhilarated by a particularly grand seasonal panorama or a small, but significant, seasonal indication? Observation of the seasons and response to them inspired all the poems you are about to read.

Watch the natural changes, the signs of the seasons: the first change of color, a new smell, a quickening or slowing of activity. These are the material for poetry.

We begin at the new beginning, spring.

Spring

As a subject for poetry, spring has a good deal going for it. Although the signs of spring may be more dramatic in northern climates, they are visible everywhere in the blooming of eucalyptus or apple trees, of cactus or trillium. The first signs of spring suggest a quickening, a renewal. We see plants and animals that weren't there just a day or two ago. The wind is different now; there are new, wet fragrances, a sense of something happening, of movement. We feel a sense of light, lightness, freedom, perhaps of nostalgia.

Mark was a third grader when he wrote "Spring." He was part of a group of about fifty children from a school I had never visited before. I knew none of the children before me, but we had a task to accomplish together. It was mid-May in northern Minnesota, and we could see that spring was finally a reality. We were going to write about that reality. Since none of the children had creative writing experience, I asked their teachers to stay and to write along with us if they wished. I assured them at the outset that we were more interested in lively written expression than in perfect spelling. This is what was written on Mark's paper.

Spring flose
in the sky
and the spring rain
jumps to plas to plas
like the mice.
— Mark, age 8

If I had been in doubt about any of the words, I would have asked Mark to explain. But I knew exactly what his poem said and could hold it in my hand and read it aloud to his admiring fellow third graders.

One critic mentioned that "from place to place" would sound better than "to place to place." Mark responded seriously, "I'll think about it." I don't know what he finally did. He and the other children each made a copy of their hour's work for me and a copy for themselves. The one I own is Mark's original draft.

Here are some more spring poems by children in other settings. Katie, like many poets before her, sees spring as a beginning.

A Beginning of a New World

Spring is like a beginning
of a new world.
When the flowers open,
they open one by one.
They seem like they would last
forever.
Baby birds chirp
on their nests,
while their mother
brings a worm.
The snow melts
so much that the city
looks like Venice!

— Katie, age 11

Susan, the nonreader who earlier in the year insisted rightly that *swaggers* was a word, fell headlong into a poems-must-rhyme trap of her own making and offered this.

Spring is here
and summer is near.
Winter is far,
And we'll sing about a star.

— Susan, age 10

The class came down hard on Susan's poem. But first they pointed out that she could really write interesting things and quoted her "rain swaggers across the street" poem. Only then did they criticize the singsong rhyme and offer the opinion that " '. . . and we'll sing about a star' is crazy."

Early in the year, Susan would have lashed out at her critics. Early in the year, she would have said, "Everyone picks on me. They hate me." But now Susan merely picked up her poem and regarded the others serenely. "OK," she said, "rhyming is a big pain anyway. I don't know why I messed with it. None of them good words rhyme." Certainly "none of them good words" like *swagger*, do.

There are plenty of good words in Judy's poem about Lake Superior in a springtime mood.

A Whirly Twirly Lake

The waves of a whirling lake
move swiftly
to and fro.
Waves thrash against the rocks
like a bull charging.
They turn
and toss
and swirl
and bend.

— Judy, age 11

". . . to and fro" is probably a cliché. But there are other words, like *thrash, charging, toss, swirl,* and *blend,* which make this poem a vivid picture of a large lake on a windy spring day. Judy has caught on to the secret of good writing; she knows how to look and look and look for the right word, how to say to herself, "What else means the same as. . .?"

George was only five when I heard him sing the following little spring chant. It ends with a Minnesota child's logical instructions for helping spring hurry up, in a state where one can feel warm wind, see tulips budding, while there are still patches of stubborn snow everywhere.

> The wind is blowing
> and your tulips
> will be coming up.
> It will be time
> to ride in a wagon.
> When the wind blows again,
> the birds will be out
> in their nestes.
> Where is the spring?
> Spring will come
> if you will turn on
> the outside waterfaucet
> and squirt the water
> on the snow.
> And then you will see
> the summer grasses.
> — George, age 5

Tulips bloom in this spring haiku, and the metaphor is partly embroidery.

Garden
Tulips, ric-rac round
   daisies embroidered center,
      carnation napping.
         — Sue M., high school

Does "powdered puff" give you a different impression from "powder puff"? Read the next poem and see which you like best.

Yellow fuzzed ball
Atop a plant stem,
White powdered puff,
Blowing in the wind . . .
   Dandelion!
         — Shelly, high school

The poems and images on spring you have been reading in this chapter avoid over-used phrases and worn out concepts and, instead, let us hear the many, individual voices of children.

Op Art! Pop Art! On wing!
Bursting faith!
Dawn
      of
         Spring!
         — Shelly, high school

Children can write spring poems at any time of the year. Have your students think about what happens around them in spring. Think about spring words. Fill your chalkboard with the sights, sounds, and colors of spring. Use the mystery box. Write spring cinquains and haiku. Write spring poems when the winter doldrums hit your classroom. But especially write spring poems at the height of the season when everyone can observe firsthand the wonders of spring.

The last spring poem was written by a high school student who signed it Anonymous.

the
dimpled dew-dawn
   s l i d e s
     in on the
new-blown wind
leaking
   t
     h
       i
          n
           l
             y
               down the
                  greenly stalk
                  of
spring
while
we
  are burnt by the
    summersoon sun.

And so, spring turns into summer.

Summer

For many of us, summertime is the highlight of all the seasons. We wait for summer when we will have more time to observe and enjoy the world around us. Colors deepen and flare in summer gardens; the sounds of certain birds and insects have come to mean summer to us. The noise of a screen door slamming, the smell of newly cut grass, the splash of swimmers, the murmur of a distant radio, the feel of bare feet on hot cement —

all add up to the lazy, shimmering days of summer.

An artist uses particular colors to paint a summer scene. Look at paintings by the French impressionist Renoir. His paintings seem to exist in sunny, warm gardens or on dreamy June rivers with the very essence of a summer day reflected in the light, the air, the skin of the people he puts into his pictures.

Since an artist uses a piece of canvas as a base and colored paints as a medium, the colors themselves must suggest summer sun, breezes, heat, and flower gardens to us. Writers, too, use color to suggest summer. They use color words that can be seen vividly in the mind's eye.

Think of colors. Which ones would you choose to describe a summer scene? Are some colors warmer than others? Can some colors be downright hot? If you list colors in certain clusters, does their mood and intensity change? Look at the following descriptions and notice how many of the words show us a color. Does the first scene feel warm to you? How would you rewrite it if you wanted to make the reader feel cool?

Heat

I saw a copper bowl in a copper-color room.
In the bowl were some oranges and bananas.
Nice ripe ones. A blue and white canary in
a very gold cage — singing melody that made me
hot.
The table that the cage was on had a lot of
dandelions on top.

— Marlene, age 11

Calling her scene "A Hot Pacific Day," Katie wrote the following piece.

The toucan and parrots fly in the melting
sun. The goldenrod is sagging in the sun's
blaze. The tired old tiger yawns lazily

to take a nap, while the flamingo cools his feet in the water. The wilting poppy is dropping very low. The whole island is damp and sweaty.

— Katie, age 11

Look at the words again. Katie speaks of tropical animals and birds: *toucan, parrots, tiger, flamingo.* She uses *melting* to describe the sun, and *blaze* to emphasize its heat. Look at her wonderfully tired words: *sagging* and *wilting.* Katie scarcely needs to tell us that "the whole island is damp and sweaty." We can almost feel its heat and humidity.

In her description of a pond entitled "Quiet," Anne uses color words that we usually think of as cool — *green, blue, silver;* yet there is the warm, still feeling of a summer evening turning into a summer night. What words do you think help give this impression?

Pebbles are slimy with age. The pool is like a mirror. You look and see a greenblue pattern of stone. Everything is quiet — a sleepy quiet. A little ways off, a tired, droning bee buzzes. Night shadows fall and the pond turns silver, and quiet pebbles go to sleep.

— Anne, age 12

What happens if you remove the words ". . . a tired, droning bee buzzes"? Does the air cool? Try it.

All of the following poems, written quickly one afternoon by third graders, were simply a fast exercise in the use of color words and strong, hot verbs. In spite of many sessions stressing the use of interesting beginning words, the children began their poems with "The

Sun. . ." Generally, as a teacher, I try to encourage more
diversified beginnings.

> The sun is a lemon,
> A lemon ball.
> It rolls through
> The blue-white hall.
> > — Helen, age 8

> The sun is bright with its
> Glitter light.
> It blinds you
> When you look up.
> It's steaming hot
> When the colors are red.
> > — Jerri, age 8

> The sun is like a
> Roasted bun
> And all the girls and boys
> Come to see
> How it turns red!   and yellow!
> > — Marnell, age 8

It is hard to imagine feeling hotter than this poem.
The universe seems to be on fire.

> Beating —
> the sizzling hum of heat
> > burns my brow.
> As the ashes steadily sink
> through the sky —
> > I die.
> > > — Nancy, age 16

A dry Micronesian season brings forth this cry for relief from the heat.

> Oh rain, come to earth and wet our
> souls, for we have thirsted since your
> love has left us with Mother Earth.
> — Sulikau, age 16

Osiaol, also from a Micronesian island, wrote: "It seems that we are living in a desert now. Our land is dried up and the plants are all wilted." And she ends with, "Let me just suck my saliva." Quick, somebody, water!

When my daughter, Jane, was seven, she imagined a squirrel on a hot day. She wrote, "His fur was like strings because he was sweating." And as a fifth grader, she wrote this summer haiku.

> Bees surround the fence.
> Honeysuckle tree in bloom,
> counting the flowers.
> — Jane, age 10

On that same day, Jane's friend Alison thought of words to describe the slow movement of a sailboat and came up with one of those images that all poets look for, one that "astonishes and delights."

> Sailboat:
> Snail-walking
> toward the west,
> its sides shine
> with the sun
> on them.
> — Alison, age 11

Flowers too can bring to mind the heat of summer, as they do in this next poem.

Oriental Poppies
Flaming torches! They flash and sputter a
consuming fire
on gardens already scorched
and bare.
— Cathy, age 16

There is also about summertime a sense of faraway sounds, muted perhaps by the very heat itself which almost visibly hangs in the air. Perhaps summer seems blurred and slow to us because we ourselves are moving slowly, half-hearing summer sounds, seeing life around us as if it were a silent film in slow motion. In her poem, "Picnic," a high school writer describes just such a summer state. Listen to the effect of *glued, dull, cottoned.* . .

Picnic (a shortened version)

A ghostly throng glued to
merry-go-round,
green picnic table,
barbecue pit.

Dull crash, cottoned shout,
everyday,
holiday bare . . .

Who has heard the sun
singing quietly . . .
humming to the hazy tune
of the animals' stream? . . .

The crack of a dry twig, broken,
re-echos in the air,
the sound finished
by a cloud and a tree.
—Clarice, age 16

Write summer poems in your classroom at any time of the year, especially if you aren't in class during the summer. Use long, winter afternoons to imagine what summer would be like, were it ever to come again. Fill your chalkboard with a myriad of summer words, hot words, colorful words, wet words. And have your students write their own pictures of summer.

Autumn

Descriptions of autumn can easily become trite and shopworn — even more easily than descriptive poems about spring. We are tired of the word *falling*, whether it refers to leaves or snow. There must be other words to tell us how things fall. What are they?

Leaves are colored in the autumn. What color? Red? Like what? What else? Another word for yellow? What does it make you see? How do leaves change their colors? Use these questions and others to find new, unusual words to be used in autumn poems.

What strong verbs show how leaves pile up? How the wind blows? How the air changes?

Red leaves flutter,
Yellow ones fall.
Brown leaves gather,
All along the wall.

— Debbie, age 10

Debbie's poem has a fine word in the third line. *Gather*, used in an unusual and accurate description, saves the whole poem.

The fall winds blow in each of the three lines of this haiku.

> Scarlet leaves flying,
>   hither and thither they go,
>   scattering autumn.
>
> — Linda G., high school

The idea that leaves can scatter autumn is a departure from the concept that wind scatters leaves. This departure really makes the poem. The other two lines show movement but in much more conventional language.

This next poem belongs to Leslie M. (You may remember her amazingly good haiku from the haiku chapter.) By the time she wrote this she had learned to handle rhyme like a pro.

Against a Whitened Birch

Against a whitened birch,
A firey flash of red
swirls in the rushing wind
five feet above my head.

Is it a flaming torch?
Is it a burning fire?
Or is it a branch
of scarlet leaves
falling to the mire?

> — Leslie M., age 11

Just look at the sophisticated use of words: *whitened, firey, flash, swirls, rushing, wind.* This autumn tree is no prosaic birch; it is the burning bush. One can only hope Leslie has continued to write poetry.

> Watch out the window
>   Eery wind tarnishes —
>   Leaves . . . gold . . . remember.
>
> — Sue M., age 15

That is a marvelous idea, the autumn wind *tarnishing* the gold leaves, the leaves that can remember being gold.

In Kelly's magical poem, Indian summer is full of the perfume of apples and the glory of that last warm wind.

> Autumn
> apple-breathed
> me
> tickling me
> with leaves —
> and laughed
> color
> on an
> unsuspecting
> world —
> feigning
> to just
> wing sunshine.
>
> — Kelly, high school

Winter

Winter in the far north, where all of the poems in this section were written, is more than a season; it is a six or seven months way of life. As a subject for creative writing, it is without limit. For myself, I believe if I had to choose one word to write about for the next life-time or so, I would choose *snow.*

Winter holds every mood from the ecstasy of the first snowfall to the despair of never ending March, and words exist to describe each mood. Because I taught mainly in California, the winter section in this chapter is thin. However, students and poets from all parts of the country can write about winter — the seasonal changes in their particular climate, the snow and ice of northern climates, the moods connoted by these cold, cold images.

For the northerner, winter can be gray, white, and black — stark, like an etching. It can be enameled blue sky, blinding snow glare, and cobalt shadows. It can be soft dove gray, with white flakes hypnotically falling and falling. Northern winters have more silences than sounds, more challenges than easy times.

How would you express the temperature, the quality of the winter air? Are there words that mean the same as cold? What are they? Does coldness have a sound? A smell? Does ice have color? What are snow colors? What are snow textures? Can you think of another word for *soft*? For *fluffy*? What kinds of jewels (besides diamonds) can we talk about? Have you ever seen pink snow? When is it pink? If you have never seen snow, what have you seen to describe what you imagine snow to be like? Tell us about the winter sun. What words best describe it on a partly sunny day when the temperature is twenty degrees below zero?

Try answering all of these questions in writing with your young poets. Brainstorm for winter words and write them on the chalkboard. Then write winter poems.

Judy, age ten, uses an icy image for the sky on a day when the sun is brilliant and the temperature is thirty below zero. ". . . the blue sky was glazed," she tells us. And Katie describes what it feels like to be caught in a real blizzard.

There is nothing but snow. My hands are getting so numb they are turning blue. When I think of home, I get colder.

Now a storm is coming up. Snow is spinning and swirling around me. The snow looks like diamonds dancing in a wonderland of blackness.

— Katie, age 11

In seventeen syllables, winter haiku tells the story of this coldest season.

Snow hurling at me
    like a cloud of silver-white,
        lightly covering.

— Lisa M., high school

Look at the strong image in the second line of this next poem.

The icing sleet storm
    Blew the neighborhood jagged —
        Bits and pieces flew.

— Kay M., high school

Finally, Cathy gives us something to think about.

Winter is a chain locked on my foot,
And long after winter has gone,
Its impression remains.

— Cathy, high school

When Dan was in ninth grade the school assignment was, "write a Christmas poem." Dan adored computers about as much as he disliked writing poems, so he decided to program an imaginary computer with Christmas words and then record the result.

Sparkle, holly, merry, golden,
Twinkle, gleaming, crimson, streaming,
Glowing, watchful, starry, waiting,
Hurry, supper, presents, wrapping,
Joy, gay, happy, bouncy,
Crack, smash, tinkle, broken,
Shock, quiet, anger, mad,
Tired, sleepy, drowsy, bed
Warm,
    snug,
       peace.

— Dan, age 14

A most satisfying way to harmonize modern technology with the spirit of the season!

Bibliography

(Spring)

Conkling, Hilda. "Weather." In *Poems by a Little Girl*. Philadelphia: J. B. Lippincott Company, 1920.

Lewis, Richard, ed. "Spring." In *Miracles: Poems by Children of the English-Speaking World*, pp. 27-40. New York: Simon and Schuster, Inc., 1966.

Mathews, Jack. "The Thaw." In *The Wind Is Round*, edited by Sara Hannum and John T. Chase. New York: Atheneum Publishers, 1970.

Sandburg, Carl. "Blossom Themes." In *Wind Song*. New York: Harcourt Brace Jovanovich, Inc., 1960.

Snyder, Gary. "Sixth-Month Song in the Foothills." In *The Wind Is Round*, edited by Sara Hannum and John T. Chase. New York: Atheneum Publishers, 1970.

(Summer)

Kinnell, Galway. "In Fields of Summer." In *The Wind Is Round*, edited by Sara Hannum and John T. Chase. New York: Atheneum Publishers, 1970.

Lewis, Richard, ed. "Summer." In *Miracles: Poems by Children of the English-Speaking World*, pp. 75-84. New York: Simon and Schuster, Inc., 1966.

Sandburg, Carl. "Bee Song." In *Wind Song*. New York: Harcourt Brace Jovanovich, Inc., 1960.

(Autumn)

Booth, Philip. "Cider." In *The Wind Is Round*, edited by Sara Hannum and John T. Chase. New York: Atheneum Publishers, 1970.

Levertov, Denise. "The Willows of Massachusetts." In *The Wind Is Round*, edited by Sara Hannum and John T. Chase. New York: Atheneum Publishers, 1970.

Lewis, Richard, ed. "Autumn." In *Miracles: Poems by Children of the English-Speaking World*, pp. 119-132. New York: Simon and Schuster, Inc., 1966.

Stoutenberg, Adrien. "Companions." In *The Wind Is Round*, edited by Sara Hannum and John T. Chase. New York: Atheneum Publishers, 1970.

(Winter)

Booth, Philip. "The Total Calm." In *The Wind Is Round*, edited by Sara Hannum and John T. Chase. New York: Atheneum Publishers, 1970.

Lewis, Richard, ed. "Winter." In *Miracles: Poems by Children of the English-Speaking World*, pp. 183-194. New York: Simon and Schuster, Inc., 1966.

Moore, Lilian. "Winter Dark," "Snowy Morning," "Night Snow." In *I Thought I Heard the City*. New York: Atheneum Publishers, 1969.

Sandburg, Carl. "Winter Gold." In *Wind Song*. New York: Harcourt Brace Jovanovich, Inc., 1960.

Wilbur, Richard. "Stop." In *The Wind Is Round*, edited by Sara Hannum and John T. Chase. New York: Atheneum Publishers, 1970.

In All Kinds of Weather

There's no need to say that everyone talks about the weather; we all know that's true. Not only does everyone talk about the weather at hand, but many of us can't seem to go to bed at night without listening to a weather forecast — to find out what kind of a day occurred in places remote from us and to see what weather we can expect in the next twenty-four hours.

As an idea starter for writing, weather is a natural. Children seem to vibrate with imaginative interest in all kinds of weather. They can spend a year using the daily weather conditions as well as the more dramatic weather manifestations for subject matter. Weather poems can be straightforward descriptive scenes. Or children can write about weather as seen by animals, birds, insects, old people, young people, people in various occupations, in various parts of the world. What action words tell us about today's weather? What color words show us a picture of today?

As you read the poems that follow, imagine for yourself how you could present the same theme in two or three different ways. Consider printing your next publication of the children's writing solely on the topic of weather and including materials produced from a science unit on weather. It's a way to make science interesting for the nonscientific student who enjoys writing, and to make writing interesting for the student who favors science.

Let me again urge you to handle matters of spelling and punctuation in the most relaxed way possible. In the first bubbling out of creative juices, nobody wants to have their ideas red-penciled. Students can correct and polish later when they realize that their writing will be published and that clarity is needed to communicate the poem.

Rain

Is it raining? Rain poems are especially fun to write when there's a storm raging outside or when a steady drizzle keeps everyone inside. But they are equally satisfying to conjure up on a sunny day, especially a hot, sunny day. Whether it's raining or not, start by filling the chalkboard with rain words.

Let's talk about the sounds of rain. Ask the children what they hear on a rainy day. If someone obliges by bringing up pitter patter, explain that this is an overworked expression. If rain really sounds like pitter patter, what else does it sound like?

Terry has her own variation on that overworked sound of rain. Her rain goes "plitter platter." Albert writes that the rain on his roof says "toc — toc — toc."

Let your ears hear noises only a rain-slicked day can bring. Do you hear cars going by? What special sound do the car's tires make on wet pavement? Is there a strong word for that sound? Can that sound be compared to something else? In the following poem a third grader succinctly describes the sound car tires make.

When the cars
Run over the rain,
It slaps the sidewalk.
— Joe, age 8

His twin brother Tom said it this way.

When it rains
It storms and pours
And the cars going by
Seem like their tires
Are split in two
By rain.
— Tom, age 8

". . . tires . . . split in two by rain" really lets us hear the ripping sound of tires on a wet street.

When eliciting responses about the sound of rain from children, we can ask, "Is there any musical instrument you think of when you imagine rainy noises?" Wolfram heard a small, tinkling instrument and wrote this poem.

When the rain came down
In the dark day
It came down
Like little bells tinkling.
It clattered like little rocks.
— Wolfram, age 10

Beverly thought of thunder as a drum. She had a fine first line one day, but she couldn't get anywhere with it. So we put it on the chalkboard for the third grade to share. "The drumbeat of thunder" was now everybody's possible first line. After an afternoon of intermittent interest in that one line, Barry wrote a second line that the class approved of. We added his line to Beverly's.

The drumbeat of thunder
Is pounding away

Interest was immediately revived. Everyone began looking for a third line. When Robert offered his suggestion, "on the dead white steeples," the debate was hot and furious. Most of the class felt that "dead steeples" were "too spooky." (Their teacher thought privately that it was a wonderfully strange image!) Reluctantly, Robert changed the image to "high steeples" and then added another line to finish the poem. Here is the finished poem.

> The drumbeat of thunder
> Is pounding away
> On the high, white steeples
> Over the bay.

I've included this example of another kind of group effort to illustrate the ongoing interest which can be generated in a classroom where the opportunity to work and play with words is constant and where an individual's efforts at expression are seriously regarded by student and teacher alike.

Suppose rain is a person. Can you imagine this rain? How does it move? Where does it go? What is rain wearing? Is rain a man? A woman? Old? Young? Susan personified rain in this poem.

> Rain skips across
> The alleys of the world
> The rain swaggers across
> The street . . .
>
> — Susan, age 10

Here is another way of seeing the rain as a person.

> Every time
> When it is raining hard
> and you are in your house
> and the rain splashes on your roof,
> It sounds like a man is on your roof,
> and it sounds like he is hammering a nail
> on top of your roof.
>
> — Peggy B., age 9

What do you see on a rainy day? Are there colors
in the rain? What colors can you see? Are there colorful
wet things that show up in the rain? What are they?

Ann made up the following rainy day word picture.

> The colors of rain
> Are like a rainbow in the sky.
> The cars have a SWASH as they go by.
> The people in their yellow raincoats go by.
> As they walk
> A wiggly shadow is behind them.
> The rain on the rooftop
> goes pitter patter
> all day long.
>
> — Ann, age 8

The triteness of the phrase "pitter patter" is more than
offset in this poem by the other language. Not only can
we see the people in their "yellow raincoats," but we can
also see their "wiggly shadows" distorted by the rain.

Suppose rain had a hardness to it, like gem stones.
What would hard rain be like? The word *diamonds* occurred to one of the third graders I was working with.
After taking its place on our chalkboard, it appeared in
several poems. Here is one of them.

> One day the rainbow
> Slashed across the sky
> With a gold, silver, and copper sparkle.
> It looked like little diamonds.
>
> — Corinne, age 8

Notice the strong word *slashed* in this poem; it allows
us to see the knife-edged rainbow Corinne saw in her
imagination.

And Susan, age ten, says that the rain "twinkles
and sprinkles crystally in the sky like diamonds on a
bride." Susan made her comparison of rain to diamonds

especially effective by her twin verbs "twinkles and sprinkles" and her invented adverb *crystally*.

Here is a rain poem with a little different kind of hardness to it.

> Crystal wires of rain
> Capture me
> then shatter. Freedom!
>
> — Ann N., high school

How does rain move? Ask the students for some good, lively words for the way rain moves along the street, over puddles, against windows, through trees. The word *skips* appeared on our chalkboard. It appealed to Susan, Richard, and to other children as well.

Here is Richard's poem.

> Thunder walks
> through the rain
> and lightning skips
> lightly by.
>
> — Richard, age 9

Thunder takes its time. We can hear it walking through the rain. And the "lightning skips lightly by" faster than thunder and not nearly so noisy. These are extremely apt images.

See the animals in the wet outdoors. See their fur, their ears, their reflections in streets, puddles, windows. How do animals feel about rain? Do cats and ducks have the same feeling about rain? Imagine you are an animal in the rain. If you were an animal, how would the rain make you feel?

Think about plants. See the rain on petals, dripping off leaves, bending stems. Is there a special smell the wet earth gives off? Can you find words for that damp, mossy fragrance? Nancy wrote a haiku to describe the aftermath of a spring shower.

> Each wet tulip cup
>   Tosses its head, pouring out
>   Cloud-pitchers of rain.
>   — Nancy W., age 14

Think about puddles. Can you see children and puddles? Look hard at those children as they run through the puddles. What do children running through puddles sound like? Think of some strong action words to describe a child's feet meeting a puddle.

Think about puddles and rain, with no children in sight. Does this poem let you see a puddle in a new way?

> When the raindrops fall
> on a puddle,
> They look like shooting-stars
> In the blue mud-puddle sky.
>   — Elvira, age 10

This poem has the fresh sound and impact of real poetry. I don't believe I've ever read "blue mud-puddle sky" before. Have you?

Wind

An invisible force, the wind has always stirred imaginations of writers. The push and shove of moving air is a theme with endless variations. No matter where we live, wind is a common experience.

So ask your students, "What does the wind do?" The word that comes to everyone's mind is *blow!* And it goes up there on the chalkboard to begin the torrent of wind words that will appear as the children start to think. But what else means blow? Think of a word that means to blow very hard. Someone says *rage;* another suggests *sweep;* still another offers *rushes.* These are

good words that go on the chalkboard to join the others.
Following are three poems that use the word *rushes*.

The wind
Rushes your kite
and tears your kite
and pushes your kite!
— Roger, age 8

The wind rushes to the sun
And takes his place.
— Gaynell, age 8

The wind rushes across
the green meadows.
It blows my hair
Like purple thistles
In the sky.
It blows my dress and petticoat
like dry leaves
Sailing high.
— Elvira, age 10

Jerry lets us hear all sorts of wind noises in this
picture of kites.

Kites are in the air.
When the wind blows against the kites
It cracks the kites.
And it tears and rips the kites
to pieces.
Winds blow as hard as a fan.
The wind whistles and roars as loud
as thunder.
— Jerry, age 8

Look at those snapping, strong words — *cracks, tears, rips* — and see what they do for the poem. They are all short, striking words with hard consonant sounds. This is not a gentle wind.

In this next poem the wind is also tearing.

When the kites are in the air
it seems like the wind stops the kites
from flying.
When the wind blows
it looks like the wind
tears the leaves
off the trees!

— Joe C., age 9

Is there color in the invisible wind? Young poets say there is indeed.

There is a silver wind
It would push you down
Orange wind at sunset,
Because it's so nice,
That's why.

— Jerry, age 8

107   *In All Kinds of Weather*

Beverly sees the wind as both a color and a shape.

> The wind is a copper shape
> And it rolls and rolls
> Till it is a bowl.
>
> — Beverly, age 9

Think about the smell of wind. What does it depend upon? Can we guess where the wind has been by breathing it?

> If you went by a bakery
> When the wind was blowing,
> The wind would smell like
> Baker's hot bread,
> Hot buns,
> Hot cakes.
>
> — Jerry P., age 8

The following poem originated in a seacoast town in northern California.

> I went outside with my kite
> And the wind smelled
> Like salt
> That came from the sky.
>
> — Audrey, age 10

Kim used the idea of saltiness too, but in a different way.

> The kite glides across the sky
> with a swishing noise.
> The sky is full of
> many fish.
> The fish fly across
> The salty sky.
>
> — Kim, age 8

Now stretch your mind again. Think of the wind as a person. Who is this windy fellow? Or is it a woman you see blowing about? What does the wind wear? How old is the wind? What does wind do? What does it use? Emily Dickinson wrote that "the wind tapped like a tired man," and Carl Sandburg spoke of a spendthrift wind that walked through an apple orchard "counting his money and throwing it away." How do you see the wind? Strong? Kind? Mean? The following poems show how some children personified the wind.

> The trees bow low
> When the wind rides by,
> Because they know
> He's King of the Sky.
> — Vickie, age 8

Vickie's wind has a dash of grandeur about him.

> The wind is like an old man
> and he blows softly
> Over the sun.
> — Ronnie, age 9

Here is a teasing wind.

> Oh, oh! My hat!
> The wind has stolen
> My hat!
> I can't get it.
> Now I have it,
> And the wind laughs at me.
> That was a big joke!
> — Margo, age 9

In the following bit of prose, called "The Ages of Wind," the wind is also personified.

The wind sweeps across the earth like a poised young princess, thrashes itself against cold brownstone buildings, spins like a used top, and ends like an old woman staggering on the top of a hill.

— Mary S., age 12

And Anne L., age ten, wrote, "The fingers of Wind are curling around defenseless trees."

This next poem has a misty feeling that is lovely, and the last line is an unusual description of birds.

It is a windy night and
    a stormy night
and the dusk is all around,
In the air,
and on the northern
    plains of Minnesota.

High in the air, the wind is rough
and the fog is the mist of
    the hills.
The birds fly around in the air
Trying in vain
To find their homes,
With their wings of rain
and their bodies of wetness.

— Jane, age 10

Every once in a while, a poem "wants to rhyme" and we let it. Emily had a tendency, at age eight or nine, to think in rhyme, but her poems often avoided that deadly "moon-spoon-June" writing of children. Her awareness of the power of words is revealed in the following poem.

The Wind

The wind is quite a lively thing,
Carrying tunes that bluebirds sing,
Howling, whistling, soaring away
Off to the shores of the sparkling bay.
When he gets angry,
Waters splash.
As he begins to fight and lash,
Leaves go flying through the air,
Crackling, swishing
Here and there!

— Emily, age 9

Emily uses *soaring* and *lash* like an old pro — and with excellent results.

Here then, you have the wind, as seen by children. Constant searching for the right word, the new comparison, the fresh image will help you and your students create a sweeping windstorm in your classroom too. We expect it to blow away the cobwebbed phrases and mildewed, overworked ideas forever!

Third Grade Weather Myths

During a unit on weather, California third graders grew most knowledgeable about the water cycle; the reasons for snow formations and rainfall; the theories behind light refraction and rainbows. Along with their scientific probings, they read many myths and legends from ancient peoples who also sought to explain these same phenomena.

Quite naturally, the children began inventing their own tales to explain to their "people" the frightening and mysterious natural happenings around them. The following prose selections are some of the *Stories of Magic Reasons* that resulted from their interest in science and their delight in writing.

The Legend of the Stamping Horse

Once, many, many years ago, there lived
a horse. No one could catch the horse because
it was the horse of lightning. Every time men
tried to catch the horse it ran so fast that it made
lightning!

Then one day the horse was caught. Famous
horse trainers came and they found out that
this horse was the stamping horse of lightning.

The men called to the men at the stall,
"Open the gate." And they opened the gate
and suddenly the sky blackened and lightning
roared.

And then ALL the men knew that
this running horse was the horse of lightning.

— Roger, age 9

The sky is strange. The snow crystals have
six points on them. The lightning devil is very
mean. He only comes out when it is stormy.
His horns are very hot and red and his tail
is sharp as an arrow and his body is like fire.
He is red all over except his eyes: they are
YELLOW and RED!

— Mike, age 8

Lightning and Thunder

Once a man had some lightning in one of
his hands and thunder in his other hand.
His name was Adad and this was long ago.
He was angry all the time. He was not a
good man at all. He would throw his thunder
around. The people did not like him at all.
He had long hair too. It was very long.
When he goes by people, he throws his thunder.
— Leanne, age 8

The Buffalo Herd

Once upon a time some Indians were
going hunting. They saw some buffalo. The
Indians began to chase the buffalo. When
the Indians shot a buffalo, lightning came
out of their horns. So every time you see
lightning you will know why.
When the buffalo fell it thundered.
When they ran it thundered too.
— Chris, age 9

The Wind

Once upon a time there was a man who told
fairy tales about the wind. He said that
the wind was a witch sweeping her floor with
her broom in the air. That made the wind
blow real hard and her hands can make wind
go fast and makes trees go back and forth.
And she can make it stop too. The wind is
dangerous because it can make a tidal wave in
the ocean. You cannot see the wind but it
can feel you all the time.
— John, age 8

The Snow and Its Magic

Once upon a time there was a train. And it carried horses high in the sky. But these are secret horses. Do you know what they do? When they throw back their manes the jewels flutter down to earth. So that is why there is snow.

— Kim, age 8

What causes the weather? Ask your students!

Bibliography

Bishop, Elizabeth. "Electrical Storm." In *The Wind Is Round*, edited by Sara Hannum and John T. Chase. New York: Atheneum Publishers, 1970.

Colum, Padraic. "I Saw the Rain Today." In *The Golden Journey: Poems for Young People*, edited by Louise Bogan and William J. Smith. Chicago: Reilly and Lee Company, 1965.

Dickinson, Emily. "The wind tapped like a tired man." In *Modern American Poetry and Modern British Poetry*, edited by Louis Untermeyer. rev. ed. combined ed. New York: Harcourt Brace Jovanovich, Inc., 1962.

_____. "The Storm." In *Selected Poems and Letters of Emily Dickinson*, edited by Robert Linscott. Garden City, N.Y.: Doubleday & Company, Inc., Anchor Books, 1959.

Doolittle, Hilda. "Storm." In *This Singing World: Junior Edition*, edited by Louis Untermeyer. Harcourt Brace Jovanovich, Inc., 1926.

Esbensen, Barbara J. "Storm." In *Swing Around the Sun*. Minneapolis, Minn.: Lerner Publications Co., 1965.

Hughes, Langston. "April Rain Song," "Sun Song."
In *Don't You Turn Back*, edited by Lee B. Hopkins.
New York: Alfred A. Knopf, 1969. (Original Title:
I Bring You My Songs: Poems by Langston Hughes.)

———. "In Time of Silver Rain." In *Fields of Wonder*. New
York: Alfred A. Knopf, 1947.

Lady Ise. "The Rains of Spring." In *Little Pictures of
Japan*, arranged by Olive Beaupré Miller. Chicago:
The Book House for Children, 1930.

Lewis, Richard, ed. "The Wind and the Rain." In *Miracles:
Poems by Children of the English-Speaking World*, pp.
41-60. New York: Simon and Schuster, Inc., 1966.

Moore, Lilian. "Summer Rain," "Rain Pools." In *I
Thought I Heard the City*. New York: Atheneum
Publishers, 1969.

Patchen, Kenneth. "Who Walks There?" In *The Wind Is
Round*, edited by Sara Hannum and John T. Chase.
New York: Atheneum Publishers, 1970.

Sandburg, Carl. "Summer Grass," "Wind Song," "Baby
Song of the Four Winds," "Winds of the Windy
City," "Sleep Impression." In *Wind Song*. New York:
Harcourt Brace Jovanovich, Inc., 1960.

Scollard, Clinton. "Rain Riders." In *Time for Poetry*, compiled by May Hill Arbuthnot. rev. ed. Chicago:
Scott, Foresman and Company, 1968.

Stafford, William. "Tornado." In *The Wind Is Round*,
edited by Sara Hannum and John T. Chase. New
York: Atheneum Publishers, 1970.

Young, Ella. "Rain." In *Time for Poetry*, compiled by
May Hill Arbuthnot. rev. ed. Chicago: Scott, Foresman and Company, 1968.

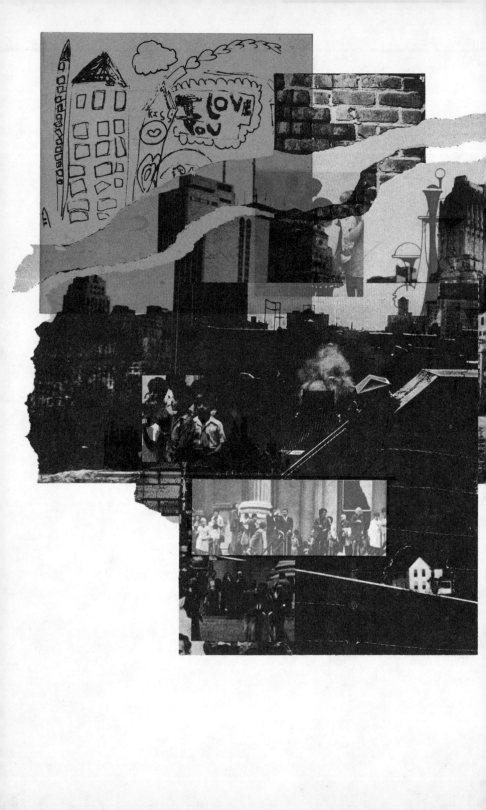

City

Today's urban community presents a rich source of ideas for writing. The poems in this book have all been written by city children and young people; but the poems included in the book thus far have mostly reflected their feelings about nature and natural phenomenon rather than their interest in the city for its own sake.

Now let's turn to the city itself, in all its complexity and variety. The possibilities for poem ideas, as we've said before, are always endless, no matter where we choose to look. The city is no exception. A quick listing of some city subjects may be helpful here.

buildings	signs and posters
noises	textures
people	building demolition
animals	construction
movement	clocks
color	steeples
lights	store windows
sun and shadow	trash cans
rain and reflections	theater marquees
snow	wires
rooftops	poles
alleys	elegance
litter	poverty
fire escapes	vehicles
personal feelings	parks
tenements	escalators
elevators	

You will no doubt add many ideas to this bare beginning. Each item on this list can, and should, suggest further images for the writer to use. Students will think of topics themselves. Encourage them to write about the parts of the city they know best. What does their neighborhood look like? Do they live in apartment buildings, houses, in the suburbs, in the city itself? Do they walk to school or take a bus? How do they see their city?

Sherry sees the city in summer. She enjoys playing with opposites in her poem.

Water, ice,
cool ponds and lakes,
blue-green water falling.
You are starving for this
on a hot city night.
— Sherry Z., age 13

The long, hot, muggy days seem one hundred times worse to city-dwellers who must live with streets, sidewalks, and sides of buildings reflecting the heat. Instead of telling us about the hot searing sun on metal and concrete, Sherry focuses on something quite different. The result is a poem about city heat that uses only cool words.

Ben's city is smog-bound, and his choice of words here is particularly effective.

Windows and buildings crusted
with sediment of progress
choking the senses with a fatal
wind-blown cloud.
— Ben W., age 15

Crusted lets us know that the dirty layers of smoke have been piling up on the windows and buildings for a long time. He uses *sediment* for the same reason. It is a word often used to describe the slow sifting of powdered rock through water. And his ironic use of *progress* is a strong choice. *Choking* and "fatal wind-blown cloud" tell it all, dramatically.

Many of the poems in this chapter were done one morning in Minneapolis by students I was meeting for the first time. The mystery box idea lends itself particularly well to the city topic, so after we talked about writing, about playing with words, and after we put many city words on the chalkboard, each of the children picked a topic from the mystery box.

You can start with the city at a particular time of day. Can you see the city at night? Its lights move or run or blink or stare, depending on your point of view. What does night hide? What do lights illuminate? How does the city by night differ from the city by day?

Carolyn places her dirty city under early morning light, before things begin their mad move and dash. Perhaps the factories are still asleep, too, for she lets us smell air that is "like fields of grass."

Dim lights
shine on the city.
Early morning
is
a magenta morning
and a gold copper morning.
Air is like fields
of grass.
— Carolyn, age 8

Look at a single building. What does it look like during the day? What does the same building look like at night?

Think about alleys. Think about corners. Think about tall buildings that block out the sky. What are the special feelings city people have when they see themselves closed in on all sides by hard, high walls? Can you describe these city feelings?

Or, think of an old, old building about to be demolished. Look, with your mind, at the scroll shapes, the fancy carving, the points and tower shapes. What has this graceful old relic seen? Can you see the new city through the eyes of an old building about to die at the hands of the demolishing crew?

What shapes do we find in city shadows? Lines? Grids? Are there triangles of shadow? What can cast a round shadow? An oval one? A zigzag shadow? When the sun is at high noon, what happens to the shadows of buildings, of people? When the sun is low in the sky, how do shadows change? Do shadows have color?

Who could name all the things there are to look at in the city? One great place to look at almost anything and everything is store windows. And Roberta's focus in this poem is on the doll-like mannequins that show off clothes.

> Posing —
> Alive or dead?
> Modeling all day long
> Standing stiff, staring at people
> all day.
>
> — Roberta, age 12

Not a real person here either, but a bridge personified, speaks the sad, lonely lines in Jolene's quiet cinquain.

> Stretching
> my strong steel bones
> across the red river,
> I'm not going to last too long . . .
> farewell.
>
> — Jolene, age 11

Here is another poem about a bridge with a very different mood.

Rivers, Boats and Bridges
Glimmering nights over the river
are very glamorous.
Boats with their lights look like
cakes with candles and bridges
look like ribbons.
— Anna L., age 9

Think about city animals. Where are we to look
for them? The city has them, of course. Think about
birds. Which ones fly free in the city? Which birds live
in cages? There are dogs and there are cats — elegant,
pampered ones and ragged, neglected ones.
Can you imagine a poem about rats? Cockroaches?
What are some rat words? Think of cockroach words.
How do rat words differ from words that make us see
and feel the *insectness* of a cockroach? Is there a difference in the weight of the words? The way they move?
Describe a rat's leg. Now describe a cockroach's leg.
Words can let us see each kind of leg. Try it!
Imagine an ant hill on a busy city street. How
are the people rushing by like the ants scurrying about
the ant hill? What do people look like to ants?
Some of the city's wild animals live in zoos. "City
Tiger" is the title of the next poem.

I
roar
and have many stripes.
I eat steak every day.
I live in a small cement cage
— and dream.
— Dejohn G., age 12

The writer said he wanted to contrast the good (steak every day) with the bad (the small cage) from the tiger's point of view; and he wanted to let us know that the tiger wishes for his own jungle home. Do you think he's achieved this? Look at the last two words. All the longings for freedom a tiger could possibly feel are summed up by " — and dream."

Nora's mystery box topic was "the zoo." She had a strange idea of who lives at the zoo — and some feelings about being caged.

The Zoo

The zoo is where some
animals stay every night and day.
But there seems to be a little
girl in a cage too.
My, my!
Is this the zoo?

— Nora W., age 9

And what about people in the city? We have a whole chapter in this book devoted to people of all kinds. When we concentrate on city people specifically, do we find some traits or attitudes that seem different from country people or people in small towns?

Even though airplanes are air-conditioned, travel is tiring, and Ann has seen the people boarding planes at a big city airport in summer. What do the words "paper people" and "cutout humans" make you see? Are the words well-chosen?

Airplane.
Sun's rays on wings —
Paper people wilting,
cutout humans are not caring
in flight.

— Ann W., age 13

Seeing the city as a lonely place, Mary Beth draws us this picture of a man whose aloneness is a symbol of the impersonal city.

The brick walls . . . with brick upon brick
following the wall,
the gray slabs
cracked with age,
old and worn.

The tops meet the gray skies
filled with swiftly fleeting clouds
as,
cold and uninviting,
the roofs of the city loom:
patches of cement fields
broken by soaring be-speckled
pigeons.
A man walks — the gray slabs
unaware —
The cement fields . . .
. . . the brick walls.

— Mary Beth, high school

The people in Tim's elevator poem seem to echo the impersonal tone of the preceding poem. We get a sense of weariness and separateness from the words "heads are hanging" and from the description of the people as they "slip off into the crowd." The poem suggested itself to Tim when he chose a new kind of mystery slip in addition to the one giving him a subject idea, *elevator*.

On this new slip was written a word that the writer must use as the first word in a poem. *Solemn* was the word that sparked Tim's mind that afternoon with the following result.

Solemn people on an elevator:
Heads are hanging
people are staring at the floor.
When the first floor comes,
they slip off into the crowd.

— Tim, age 10

If we think about the way city people move, what words come to mind? There are people on sidewalks, people in stores, in elevators, on the street, in restaurants — how do they act?

"Speedy," the sixth graders said. They *dash, push, shove, rush, run, crowd, pull, yank, jab.* Debbie imagined the Christmas rush when she wrote:

Shoving, crowded shoppers
do not
have fun
when they are in a hurry.
Christmas shopping.

— Debbie, age 12

124   *A Celebration of Bees*

At a fire, people act in certain ways, and a sixth grader tells us about them.

Red truck,
blowing siren,
people screaming, yelling!
Water spraying, people saying
Fire! Fire!

— D. M., age 12

And Joan's "Supermarket" is a frenzied place indeed.

Wide,
    big —
baskets of groceries
    and carts speeding
faster, faster —
    people run to clerk —
        zooming carts.

— Joan, age 11

But all descriptions of city people do not need to be pictures of frantic or noisy individuals. The city shows us its quiet moods too, and sounds become dulled sometimes, dull enough, perhaps, to let us hear birds call.

Alone in the Dark

I was sitting on the front porch
and I could feel
the slick and silky wind
whirl
about my shivering arms . . .
and I felt the gloomy night
coming
and the crows cawing.

— Mary B., age 10

There is a fine sense of approaching dark in that little poem.

When we consider the essence of the city, we certainly think of its sounds. "Deafening noise" was the first reaction of a group of sixth graders in an inner-city school to the question "What do you hear in the city?" The chalkboard soon resounded with *rumble, pounding, clank, scraping, clang, boom, roar, squeal, thump, squeak, sonic boom, smash, clash, crash.*

Tell about sirens, I suggested. The words came: *screaming, wailing, yelling,* a *howl,* a *red shriek,* a *white scream.*

What makes the big noises? The empty spaces on the chalkboard filled up: *jets, trucks, bulldozers, wrecking ball, sirens, ambulances, whistles, bells, cars, buses, helicopters, motorbikes, parade, street sweeper, police cars.* If you read the list aloud, you'll hear it fairly roar at you.

Every imaginable kind of motorized vehicle rumbles and sputters along city streets. In the chapter "Animating the Inanimate," we find trucks compared to ants or elephants. In the poem "Cars at Night" in that same chapter, they are animals, "released from their cages . . . blinking their eyes."

Bill's cement mixer menaces us.

Giant

. . . thundering —
crunching rock, gravel, and sand,
it moves.

— Bill, age 11

The words, "it moves" evoke a ponderous, sinister, unstoppable thing. *Thundering, crunching,* and *moves* are heavy sounds. If Bill had said *bites* instead of *crunching,* the whole poem would be lighter and quicker. Or, if he had said the machine was being driven instead of saying it *moves,* we would have lost the whole feeling of the cement mixer being ominously alive, moving by itself. Try it and see for yourself.

The machines don't move on their own though.

This next poem reminds us that people move machines, and not always wisely.

The Semi Crash

Move, move!
That's what he says.
But you don't listen. Pow!
Boxes flying, cans upsetting,
crack up!

— Sherry Z., age 13

You and your students can focus on a multitude of city images. Eric and Sherry write about garbage and trash with words that let us see, hear, and almost smell what they are picturing.

Shattering the morning,
the garbage man
is clanging the cans.
My ears will be ringing
'till I'm half deaf
before the sun comes up.

— Eric W., age 10

Sherry's plastic trash bags seem to have gone mad. Can you imagine the sky full of exploding bags?

Bursting
egg shells, potato skins
over the street,
garbage bags explode
into the sky.

— Sherry Z., age 13

"City wind" was the subject of the following poems. As the children called out their windiest words, the chalk-board began to give back poem ideas. We wrote words that mean *blow* but are fiercer: *rip, tear, shove, flatten, whip, stirs up, twisting, stings, burns.*

We spoke of city things that are moved by wind — dust, fragments of glass, papers, candy wrappers — and tried to come up with words to describe smoke in some new ways. Eric looked at our chalkboard full of wind words and added one of his own, *spores,* to describe smoke particles. The following excellent word picture is the result.

A frozen wind blows 'cross the town.
It flattens buildings and stirs up dust.
A harsh northwind blows spores of smoke
and it spreads and crinkles like papers
          on the street.
          — Eric W., age 10

Tim looks at the city through the imaginary eyes of the wind.

Broken glass in the alley,
Broken glass in the street.
I am the city wind.
I whip through slums
On a rainy day.
          — Tim, age 10

Nora wanted to write about the wind, too, and for her first word drew a slip of paper with *frantic* printed on it. I find this to be an effective way to solve the "how shall I begin . . ." problem. And it sometimes serves to introduce some new words to younger children. Nora didn't know what *frantic* meant. She could have exchanged it for another word. But after she got a sense of its meaning, she decided it was a good word for a wind poem and that she would try to use it. Here is her result.

Frantic wind
sounds like rock and roll bands,
like doors slamming.
And blowing wind
sounds like whistles,
in the bands.
— Nora, age 9

Bursting was the word Sarah picked as her first word. There is a great deal happening in her poem: "papers fly through the air," they are "bursting through the city."

Bursting papers fly through the air,
Bursting through the city in a flash!
The wind rises up and down as it blows
from street to street.
— Sarah, age 7

Action words fill this next poem too.

Twisting and twirling,
Jumping and throwing,
It stings, it burns,
It blows!
It is the city wind!
— Anna L., age 9

Sarah, a second grader, picked a subject slip labelled *fire escapes*, and a first-word slip, *muttering*. She decided to use them together, and the sudden image "muttering

fire escapes" gave her imagination a whole scenario
to share with us in this delightful poem.

> Muttering fire escapes
> pass secrets through the night.
> They whisper to the wind
> and the wind talks back
> with a
> swish
> swish
> swish.
>
> — Sarah, age 7

Have we seen the city as a diverse source for
writers? It has many faces, many sides, endless idea
possibilities. We have only scratched the surface here.
Expand the suggestions I've offered. Be specific if you
like. Name the building you are describing. Tell us who,
exactly, the person is you are writing about. Let us know
your city in a particular mood or time of day. City
children can tap these rich possibilities for a long time
to come.

Bibliography

Adoff, Arnold, ed. *Black Out Loud: An Anthology of Modern
Poems by Black Americans.* New York: The Macmillan Company, 1970.

_____. *City in All Directions.* New York: The Macmillan
Company, Inc., 1969.

Bennett, Rowena B. "Motor Cars." In *Piper, Pipe That
Song Again,* edited by Nancy Larrick. New York:
Random House, Inc., 1965.

Giovanni, Nikki. *Ego Tripping and Other Poems for Young
Readers.* New York: Lawrence Hill and Company,
Inc., 1974.

Goodnight Socrates. Film, thirty-four minutes, black and
white. Contemporary/McGraw-Hill Films.

Hopkins, Lee B., ed. *City Spreads Its Wings*. New York: Franklin Watts, Inc., 1970.

———. *City Talk*. New York: Alfred A. Knopf, 1970.

Hubbell, Patricia. "Road Paving." In *Apple Vendor's Fair*. New York: Atheneum Publisher, 1963.

Hughes, Langston. "City." In *Piper, Pipe That Song Again*, edited by Nancy Larrick. New York: Random House, Inc. 1965.

Larrick, Nancy, ed. *I Heard a Scream in the Street: Poems by Young People in the City*. New York: M. Evans and Company, Inc., 1970.

———. *On City Streets*. New York: M. Evans and Company, Inc., 1970.

Malam, Charles. "Steam Shovel." In *Reflections on a Gift of Watermelon Pickle and Other Modern Verse*, edited by Stephen Dunning, et al. West Caldwell, N. J.: Lothrop, Lee and Shepard Company, 1967.

Moore, Lilian. *I Thought I Heard the City*. New York: Atheneum, 1969.

Raffee, Burton. "On Watching the Construction of a Skyscraper." In *Reflections on a Gift of Watermelon Pickle and Other Modern Verse*, edited by Stephen Dunning, et al. West Caldwell, N. J.: Lothrop, Lee and Shepard Company, 1967.

Raftery, Gerald. "Apartment House." In *Reflections on a Gift of Watermelon Pickle and Other Modern Verse*, edited by Stephen Dunning, et al. West Caldwell, N. J.: Lothrop, Lee and Shepard Company, 1967.

Smith, William J. "The Toaster." In *Reflections on a Gift of Watermelon Pickle and Other Modern Verse*, edited by Stephen Dunning, et al. West Caldwell, N. J.: Lothrop, Lee and Shepard Company, 1967.

Swenson, May. "Southbound on the Freeway." In *To Mix with Time: New and Selected Poems*. New York: Charles Scribner's Sons. 1963.

Morning

What does the word *morning* bring to mind? Say the word; think about it: morning . . . morning . . . morning. What do you see? Think about the earliest, faintest beginnings of morning — in spring, summer, autumn, winter. How does daybreak change from season to season?

What are the colors of morning? How do the colors of night change as light comes to the sky, to the land, to the water? What color words show us a winter morning? A hot summer morning? What colors are in a rainy morning?

Let your mind's eye see morning light in the country, at the sea's edge, in the city. Think about shadow and sunlight. See corners, angles, spires, fire escapes, trucks, cars, telephone poles. See the shadows they cast in the morning sun.

What are morning's smells? Are they heavy or light? Salt breeze? Newly mown hay? Breakfast cooking?

How does morning make you feel? Do you get up early to greet the sun? Or do you bury your head under the covers? What are some words that describe how you feel in the morning?

What are the sounds of early morning, the ones you hear before you're even awake? Early birds? The garbage collector rattling cans in the alley? An alarm clock that won't shut up? Someone calling you to breakfast?

What are the sounds of a morning in winter? In the north, the sound of flocks of birds at their dawn feeding is conspicuously missing. What are some sounds that are missing from your winter morning? What do you hear instead? Now put the missing sounds into a spring morning. What does your inner ear hear?

Children have no trouble at all letting their minds respond to these exploring questions. Ask them. As you focus in more and more sharply on imaginative visions of morning, your chalkboard will fill up with suggestions, images, sound words, color words, and comparisons.

Compare morning to something else. Is it a man? A woman? An old person? A child? Is it an animal, a bird, or an insect? What kind of machine could bring us morning? Does a creature bring us morning? Does the persona of morning change with the seasons?

In the poem "Fern Hill," Dylan Thomas called morning a "wanderer white," a young man, striding the hills with a rooster on his shoulder. Do you think of morning as a strong young man? How do you see him? Why do you think he is wandering instead of sitting on a hill? If you were morning, would you choose a rooster as your companion?

In Kathy's poem we see the sun as a hearty, jovial sort of morning bringer.

Fresh white clouds gather
Together in wordless company
To meet the rising sun,
Then quickly scatter
Before its boisterous greetings.
— Kathy, high school

The next two poems compare morning with animals. In the first, we are not told what the animal is. Have you an idea?

First it comes, wild with fury
and delight. It is mad to be
held in captivity and happy
to be out. It is so happy that
it wants to stay on and on. But
the night won't let it; so after
awhile day begins to fade away.

— Janet S., age 11

In this next poem, a most unusual animal is compared to morning.

Morning's Glory
I woke up one glorious day
To see a wonderful sight
Before my eyes
Like a leaping frog
The morning impatiently
    Excitedly
Pushed away Mr. Night.

— Jean H., age 10

When Pat's "midnight birds" in this next poem turned out to be roosters, the class wondered. But she firmly left the phrase in her poem. Read it and see what you think about the "midnight birds."

Midnight birds crowed their morning call.
Bubbles dewed the earth.
Dancers rainbowed my garden —
. . . the sun burst darkness . . .

— Pat, high school

Predawn dark, the pale, early light, and day's full
burst of sun all figure in the following poems about
morning and daybreak.

> Cold and still . . . golden sun rays
> blooming out against the everlasting dark
> blue sky . . . light . . . extreme brightness.
> — Fabyan, age 20

Kim's poem thrusts us suddenly and loudly into
morning.

> You lie in bed
>   all is silent.
> Suddenly night leaves
>   And light takes its place
> Shining like a ball of fire
>   Like a parade
>   cymbals!
>   horns!
>   drums!
> You know then
>   Morning has arrived.
> — Kim, age 11

Another parade image lets us hear the vibrant
noises of day.

> **Gaiety in the Morning**
> Morning is here!
> Like coronets, snare drums
> Tooting and pounding
> Noisily bringing midday near.
> — Jean H., age 10

The notion of morning as a collection of bright sounds appealed to several of the children. A brass band was a favorite image to play with.

Morning

Morning comes like a big
parade with the brass
colored sun at the head.
The misty wind is blowing
with a gay and jolly sound.

— Mary R., age 10

The image of the "brass colored sun" is a good one. We can see and hear the brass section of the band at the head of the parade. Might this poem have been stronger if other sections of the band had followed? What instrument makes a sound like "the misty wind"? What other instruments might play in morning's parade?

In one class we explored a number of sun shapes. What is the sun anyway, besides round and yellow? Is it ever pink or green or any other color? Is it ever not round? What else is round like the sun?

Two eight year olds plucked the word *doorknob* from the list of sun shapes on the chalkboard. However the word evoked two very different images.

Daisy doorknob!
The sun
looks
as if it is
two inches
away.

— Kevin M., age 8

137   *Morning*

Morningrise
Mmmmmm — smell the flowers —
rust rose, violet blue.
Rusty rose
is a good smell
and the sun is a yellow
that no one's ever seen.
It is like a doorknob
in the sky.
I wonder —
if I opened it,
would it turn
to night?
                                    — Becky H., age 8

The sun's rays themselves become solid, stem-like in this next cinquain.

Golden,
amber rods poke
stems of spiralling light
underneath the blue grasses
of sky.
                                    — Nancy W., age 14

Nancy wrote a haiku too, to describe an early spring morning after a shower.

Each wet tulip cup
     Tosses its head, pouring out
          Cloud-pitchers of rain.
                                    — Nancy W., age 14

Have you ever known the frustration of over-sleeping? In the following poem, Janet shows us the frustration of racing from nighttime to morning's finish line — and losing.

You Dream
You dream about it all night,
dream that you will wake up
with it. Only somehow no matter
how hard you think, hope and
dream about it, it always
beats you. Day is not a
sleepy head.

— Janet S., age 11

There are sleepy, dim words at the beginning of
this next poem, and then as day comes, the words begin
to grow hard and bright and to move rapidly until the
last line.

Blackness softer than rain
Blanketed the drowsy world
And guarded it with dimly
        shining stars.
Cold sunrise
Drowned the sleeping darkness,
Flooding the unsuspecting earth
with hard, unyielding light.
Crickets scurried from
        the harsh day
To the shelter of
        cement cracks
        and rock piles
And awaited the evening.

— Kathy, high school

Of all the young people I've known, Kelly was one of
the most inventive in her use of words. She used nouns
as verbs — *lemoned*; nouns as adverbs — *sunly*; and, in

general, romped and played with the language as though she owned it.

Morning
sunly
lemoned its way
in today,
cheered on
by birds —
applauded
and kissed
by daisies —
leaving only
yellowed footprints
for afternoon
to guess.

— Kelly, high school

When Susan found an empty eggshell one morning in Wales, she wrote this poem and brought it to us, her American family, as a gift. Look at all the words she has used to show hollowness, emptiness: *nullity, cave, parting, blankness, silence, empty*. The entire poem gives an atmosphere of stillness and peace.

Awake.
See the pale blue of a morning sky,
a nullity, a purity.
A bird's egg,
shell empty,
fallen bare
to lie among dying flowers.
Vagrant scents in unsettled air
escape,
to drift in slow motion whirls.
Inside the pale cave

of the shadow -blue shell
all is smooth and white
but for traces
of the final parting:
bird from egg.
Silence in blankness
after the ebb and flow
of a delicate life.
Music of green-toned woods,
of falling water,
has left behind
a fragment of sky
taken gently
and dropped
among withered petals;
a bird's egg,
shell empty.

— Susan T., age 17

Bibliography

Dickinson, Emily. "I'll tell you how the sun rose," "The day came slow, till five o'clock." In *Selected Poems and Letters of Emily Dickinson*, edited by Robert Linscott. Garden City, N.Y.: Doubleday & Company, Inc., Anchor Books, 1959.

Harrison, Jim. "Morning." In *The Wind Is Round*, edited by Sara Hannum and John T. Chase. New York: Atheneum Publishers, 1970.

Lewis, Richard, ed. "Morning." In *Miracles: Poems by Children of the English-Speaking World*, pp. 17-26. New York: Simon and Schuster, Inc., 1966.

Thomas, Dylan. "Fern Hill." In *Golden Journey: Poems for Young Children*, edited by Louise Bogan and William J. Smith. Chicago: Reilly and Lee Company, 1965.

Night and the Moon

Night

Children's responses to darkness and nighttime range
from feelings of coziness and safety to uneasiness, awe,
fear. There is a mystery about the onset of night and
about night itself. In broad daylight, we can conjure up
night, there behind our eyes. This is possible because
our amazing minds can bring us anything we wish to
"see" and "hear."

Let's see what dark night scenes are alive behind
the clear eyes of children. First of all, we need to imagine
an absolutely pitch dark night. We cannot see a thing.
Can we feel something? Is there a sound?

What can you feel in the dark night? Think of words
that let you experience a nighttime feeling. Can we hear
night sounds? In the city the night is filled with sounds.
In the country, too. What are some city sounds? Put them
on the chalkboard.

How does a siren sound in the night? Can you see the
sound of a siren against the black night? Does the sound of
the siren have a color? Is it a soft sound? A stabbing sound?
What is night made of? Think of night as a kind of cloth.
What can the sound of a siren do to the cloth of night?
Imagine the sounds of a windy night. How do they differ
from the sounds of a still night? With ten words,
Randy describes the sounds of night in the following
poem.

A Dark Windy Night

The boat whistle blew . . .
a flower snapped . . .
A door slammed!

— Randy, age 8

143   *Night and the Moon*

Suppose we imagine night to be a person. Is it a man? A woman? What kind of clothes does night wear? Imagine what those clothes look like. Do they cling to the body? Do they float behind night? Are night's hands doing something? Night's fingers? What kind of hair does night have? What kind of eyes? Are they open? What is night doing? Is night dreaming? Is night on foot? Flying? Riding? What is being ridden? Can you see any packages or baskets? What colors do you imagine night prefers? Black? What are other names for night's favorite color?

In the following poems, night is portrayed as a person. Each poet personifies night a little differently.

As I went to bed
I heard a noise.
It was the Night Wizard!
You could hear him SWISHING
across the trees!

— Terry, age 10

Debbie's night is a horseman coming toward us.

I heard a horseman near
ride over the hill.
The moon shone clear.
The night was still.

— Debbie, age 10

Debbie's poem avoids the deadly tinkle-tankle of much rhymed verse that children write. It almost sounds like the first stanza of an old ballad. (Perhaps you or your students would like to write some more verses for it!)

Crafty Mr. Night

Crafty, creative Mr. Night
comes and steals the day's
bright light.
He comes with diamonds,
shimmering, gleaming.
Coming with velvet and looming,
Quickly, silently he drops it.
Then, the wind starts to howl
like a hooting owl.
Night begins to paint the moon.
He drops the diamonds.
Plunk! the stars appear.
Night is here.

— Jean H., age 10

In line 6, Jean uses the word *looming* in an unusual place in the sentence. When asked to explain "velvet and looming," she said, "The night is coming with velvet, and looming over day."

Think of night as an animal. What animals seem to have a night feeling about them? How does this animal, night, move? What is happening as the animal comes across the day world? How does day react? Can night

come as a bird? What insect could be night? In the poems
that follow, you will see what kinds of animals occurred
to a group of children as they stretched their minds' nets
to capture a new picture of night.

Darkness

Every day, after the sun goes down,
a new life begins.
It starts as smoothly as a snake,
as silently as a cat
with her green eye glistening.
Slowly,
      smoothly,
It stalks its prey.
Suddenly it comes —
the other life:
      NIGHT.

— Kim, age 11

Did you know
that there is a black bear
in the sky?
And when he roars,
it makes a sound
like thunder.
But he only does it
at night.

— Jeff, age 8

Night is like
A black panther
Waiting
for food.

— Randy, age 8

Lorri asks a question. Maybe she is thinking about the panther in Randy's poem.

Where does the panther live
in the dark night of sparks?
Please tell me where he stays
in the moonlight.

— Lorri, age 9

Can you see Lorri's "dark night of sparks"? Are those sparks stars? Or is there a fire? What do you see?

The next two poems which show us night's arrival also seem to animate night. Mary Beth's poem has an ominous tone to it.

Gloomy Black Night
I felt something
crouching in the dark velvet sky.
I heard the owls hooting,
and a black cat hissing.
I could feel my heart's drumbeat
and the winds howling.
I felt night creeping on.

— Mary Beth, age 10

It comes.
The owl awakes from its sleep.
He lets out a cry of fear;
Suddenly the hawks
Rise out of the fields
They all know what's coming —
Night!

— Janet, age 11

When night is used as the subject matter for poetry, many unusual images emerge. Here is an excerpt from Janet's poem, "Night Walking."

> . . . Velvety darkness
> all around me,
> the moon,
> splendored with beauty . . .
> — Janet, age 11

Splendored is a word that simply occurred to Janet, and it is just right as she has used it here. Is *splendored* a word? It is now!

In her poem, Elvira thought of the sky and its stars and compared them with a daisied meadow.

> In the night,
> the sky is clear,
> with white shooting-stars,
> like a meadow would be
> with crystal-white daisies
> in the lonely green grass.
> — Elvira, age 10

Most of us have had the experience, just before falling asleep, of a sliding sensation, as though the bed — with us as a passenger — is moving. Margie writes about this strange feeling.

> The beds move in the night
> When everybody is asleep.
> The farmer's house
> feels funny
> because it is such a
> black night!
> — Margie, age 8

Nancy's poem begins with the dark, lights up, and then goes dark again. The device of beginning and ending a poem with the same idea — sometimes with the very same word — is one that children enjoy. It gives a completed feeling to a poem and can solve the ever present problem of all poets: How can I end it?

Darkness filled the air
Suddenly it came:
An enormous lamp lighted
the sky.
The darkness was gone!
Then through the still night
Came the clouds,
Covering the moon,
Darkness returned.

— Nancy, age 10

George wrote a poem that seems to move rapidly from beginning to end.

As the moon came up
behind a tree,
a coyote howled,
a gun fired,
and a falling star blinded me
as it raced into the night.

— George, age 11

What gives this poem such speed? Perhaps this rapidity is achieved by relating several events, all happening at once: the moon is rising; we hear a coyote; a gun is shot; and we see a star fall. And look at the strong words George has used to show us that star. He says it *blinded* him as it *raced* into the night. He used those exact words to create a particular effect. He could have described the star as *bright*, and it could have *gone* into the night. Think how much dimmer *bright* would have made the star and how much slower it would have moved had the word *gone* instead of *raced* been used. When you help your students to conjure up the night, don't forget to ask for words like George's to put on your chalkboard.

You need to keep pressing your students for another, another, and yet another good word that means the same as whatever you are speaking about. As we've found again and again, children's vocabularies abound with words they know but seldom use. By the time they've been fluent speakers for a number of years, their self-expression becomes as commonplace and dull as ours. So, encourage them at an early age to quarry imaginative words and phrases. Everyone is excited when jewels of little-used speech are discovered and put on display for all to admire and use.

Continue to ask for words and more words. And continue to ask questions to draw out children's ideas. Ask questions about sound, sight, color; ask questions like those mentioned in this chapter and throughout the book. Ask the questions of yourself and your students, and encourage the children to question themselves and each other.

The Moon

Even now, with the astronauts' footsteps in its dust, the moon holds a fascination for the earthbound. As its shape changes, as it seems to sail across our night skies, the moon's magic remains.

When you evoke the moon's mystery with your students, start with the moon as we know it, as we see it from earth. Then, perhaps, you will want to explore the moon's image from a different perspective — from a space ship or a moonwalk.

Ask questions that will provoke the children's imagination. Put moon words on the chalkboard. Begin with shapes. What words mean *round*? What things are round? What things are both round and flat? Can a moon be compared with any of these things? If the moon is round like a ball, what is it made of? What metal? What jewel?

Is the moon always round? Do we ever see the whole moon? Think of the moon as it changes from night to night. Can you see the half-moon? What does it remind you of? What else? What does it look like when it is rocking on its curved edge? What are some words that mean the same as *curve*?

If you could have the moon, what would you do with it? Could you hold it in your hand? What would you do with half a moon? With a slice of moon? Think of the thinnest slice of moon you can imagine. What else is so thin and curved? The moon in one of its phases is the subject for this poem.

The Cradle

The moon is a cradle
swaying back and forth.
Inside the cradle
is a little baby star.
I guess it had fallen
from the sky.
I think I should give it back
to its mother.
Don't you?

— Jane, age 7

Do you know that the moon can move the oceans? How does the moon do this? What does the push and pull of gravity look like? What does gravity feel like to the ocean? A California nine year old used her experience with the moon's pull on the sea and wrote this poem.

The water goes
splish-splash
on the rocks,
And then the sea goes down
When the moon comes up.

— Marnell S., age 8

What color is the moon? Yellow? What are some other words for the yellow color of the moon? Is the moon always yellow? What other colors might it be? What color would it be on a summer night, a winter night, a stormy night, a clear night? Is the moon burning? What color are its flames? Do you ever see the moon during the day? What does it look like then?

See all the ways children have expressed the moon's color in the following poems.

> The moon went across the sky,
> And it is different colors, too.
> It turns to red and yellow,
> And it turns to orange
> and blue.
> — Jerry P., age 8

> The moon is yellow
> As can be.
> It's the color of gold.
> It looks like a golden locket
> Hanging from the blue neck
> Of the blue shady sky.
> — Elvira, age 10

> There is a golden moon tonight
> and all the stars
> are shining bright.
> Her eyes glitter
> like stars in space,
> and her hands and feet
> are the galaxies.
> — Edith S., age 9

Edith's moon is bright and golden, but it is also a beautiful lady with glittering eyes and twinkling hands and feet. Could the moon be a person? What would the moon as a person look like? What would its personality be?

Here's a poem with a golden moon — but with a difference.

> The moon reminds me
> of golden butter.
> It looks bright yellow,
> And when the stars come out
> at night,
> They start
> > Nibbling
> > > on
> > > > it!
>
> — Gaynell M., age 8

Barry saw a stretch of moonlight on a rug and wrote this discovery poem.

> When I was walking
> To the door,
> There sat the moon
> Glowing with gold.
> Now I know it is red,
> and blue,
> and the color
> of my floor!
>
> — Barry McC., age 8

And here is another moon color.

> When it is night
> the moon is an ivory ball.
> The owls sit on trees
> and stare at him
> with their great big eyes.
>
> — Dan, age 12

Steve sees the moon glittering on a dark night.

At night
When the night is made
of velvet
and when the moon is made
of glitter,
a shooting star will fly
through the night
faster and faster
behind a tree —
Never to see me again.

— Steve, age 11

And the shooting star sees Steve, in his poem — until it disappears.

When Katie sees the moon, she hears music.

Night Moon
I looked outside my window
and saw the round face
over my head.
The freckles of light
danced over the face.
I could hear crickets
playing in their dazzling
        new orchestra.
The owls were hooting
in their choir.

— Katie, age 12

That's what the moon looks like from earth. What if you could travel to it? What words describe the speed of a vehicle as it hurtles through black space? On the chalkboard, put all the words that mean the same as *fly*. How do you describe weightlessness? What appears through the porthole of your spaceship?

What does the moon look like from a distance? How does its appearance change as you get closer and closer? You're there! What words describe the texture of the moon's surface? How do astronauts move around on the moon's surface?

You've completed your mission, and you're leaving the moon. How does the moon look as you fly away from it? Does it get smaller and smaller? What does it remind you of?

After the initial word finding sessions, we decided to write each poem in three sections: blast off, space flight, and moon walk. However, we did each section as a separate exercise so everyone could really concentrate on that phase of their space adventure. This concentration paid off, as you will see. Notice how each section of every poem has used words that evoke the particular event being described.

Blast Off
Fire!
Ground vibrates — steam —
rocket fuel burns red flame.
It's an earthquake with hot lava —
furnace.

Space Flight
Freezing —
soundproof . . . endless.
White clouds swirling, earth blue
— silver stars burn across black —
Freezing.

Moon Walk
Deep holes
dark. Jumping
and fooling around — floating
— silver light glows in the dark —
slowly.
                                    — Tom G., age 10

Tom speaks of space as "Freezing." Yet he tells us that "silver stars burn across black," allowing us to imagine icy space filled with burning, hot suns that are stars.

Blast Off
Countdown,
high hopes, tense faces . . .
Blast off! Vibrating sounds
drowning out frightening screams —
Breathtaking.

Space Travel
Cheetah in the dark
travels to its quest
faster than sound —
whizzing through space —
only the soundless stars
seep through the darkness.

Moon Walking
Slow-motion elephants
Kicking up dirt
and leaving huge footprints
in the midnight crystals.

— Sue Van D., age 12

Sue could have called "midnight crystals" black dust, but that description wouldn't have been as effective.

Blast Off
. . . two, one
Blast Off!
Viewers watch the thrilling dive
to the moon,
Breathlessly
they await
the landing rocket.

Space Flight
Diving through space
zooming across the black,
airless sky,
the burning moon,
sparkling stars
look bigger.

Moon Walk
Meadows of black dust
cover the moon.
Astronauts
take great bounds
through craters
filled with silver rain.

— Pattie Van D., age 10

The strong, unusual images in this poem are "airless
sky," "burning moon," "meadows of black dust," and the
stunning word picture of "craters filled with silver rain."

Rocket
Vibrates —
earthquake rumble
red yellow orange fire
red flames — flares — writes like white steam
a pen.

Falling Stars
Silver
sparkling like
golden stars — falling like
cotton balls softly floating down.
Silent.

Moon Walk
Walking
over hills of
green cheese in their gray suits
floating in the air and talking —
Drifting.

— Jane G., age 8

Jane combines the scientific knowledge of today's space-age child with the old tales about the moon when she impishly speaks of the astronauts "walking over hills of green cheese."

Rocket
Blast!
The ground shrivels.
It sounds like an earthquake
flares of red, yellow, and orange fly up —
white steam.

Outer Space
Silent,
floating in space,
watching the stars fly by
an infinity of blackness —
silent.

Moon Walk
Sand puffing up
like smoke from a chimney
from the hard shoes that hit the sand.
Moon Walk.

— Caroline L., age 10

Caroline tells us, "The ground shrivels." Shrivels is exactly the right word to show us how fast the earth becomes small as the rocket takes off.

Come back down to earth. The night, the dark, the moon — use them often as subjects for lively imaginative writing.

Bibliography

Barnstone, Aliki. "The Astronaut." In *The Real Tin Flower: Poems about the World at Nine*. New York: The Macmillan Company, 1968.

Behn, Harry. "The Lake," "Two Views of Planet Earth." In *The Golden Hive*. New York: Harcourt Brace Jovanovich, Inc., 1966.

Bly, Robert. "After Working." In *The Wind Is Round*, edited by Sara Hannum and John T. Chase. New York: Atheneum Publishers, 1970.

Cornford, Frances. "At Night." In *This Singing World: Junior Edition*, edited by Louis Untermeyer. New York: Harcourt Brace Jovanovich, Inc., 1926.

Deutsch, Babette. "No Moon, No Star." In *The Wind Is Round*, edited by Sara Hannum and John T. Chase. New York: Atheneum Publishers, 1970.

Lewis, Richard, ed. "Night." In *Miracles: Poems by Children of the English-Speaking World*, pp. 195-214. New York: Simon and Schuster, Inc., 1966.

Sandburg, Carl. "River Moon," "Night," "Timber Moon," "Nocturne in a Deserted Brickyard," "Drowsy," "Nightsong," "Window," "Auctioneer." In *Wind Song*. New York: Harcourt Brace Jovanovich, Inc., 1960.

Stephens, James. "Check." In *Time for Poetry*, compiled by May Hill Arbuthnot. rev. ed. Chicago: Scott, Foresman and Company, 1968.

Teasdale, Sara. "Moon's Ending." In *Collected Poems of Sara Teasdale*, edited by Marya Zaturenska. New York: The Macmillan Company, 1953.

People and More People

Here is a subject that is without limits; people are everywhere. What makes us what we are? What makes us who we are? Are we alike? How? Are we different? How? What are people all about?

Let's begin by looking at the one person we ought to know best — ourselves. How can you sum yourself up? Can you choose words that will paint a portrait of yourself? Start by asking your students to ask questions about themselves. Encourage them to find creative ways to express the person they know best.

This is Julie's self-portrait in haiku form. What kind of girl do you see here?

A bee has this mouth,
   feeling sorry for herself —
    a bad time of day.
            — Julie C., age 10

Cathy tells us what she is in this next poem. Look at the marvelous variety of images she uses to bring us closer to her portrait.

I am a tall birch tree
with branches beginning to bend.
I am a small dog
with a coat beginning to shine.
I am Spring
just beginning to come forth,
And I am a freshly oiled door
beginning to slowly open.
            — Cathy C., high school

Sometimes it is hard at first for children or young people to get a handle on which way to describe themselves. They know so many things about themselves, but they need help with focusing their self-knowledge so that their poems can become concrete, creative works, rather than general "I am" listings.

One way to begin is to ask questions like these: What creature in the animal kingdom reminds you of yourself? What characteristics do you have that are like those of an animal, a bird, an insect?

Betsy is a nine year old with the creative ability to feel the stretch, and pull, and length of a giraffe's neck. She has obviously had some experience with sore throats as well.

I
am a giraffe.
When I get
a sore throat,
It hurts
    ten
       feet
          down.
It's a L O N G
swallow!

                — Betsy A., age 9

Two girls who see themselves as chatterers chose two very different animals for comparisons.

I feel I would be a monkey . . .
I would swing my tail. I would
chatter and chatter all the time. A
chattering monkey is what I would want to be!

                — Rae, age 9

It seems to me
that I am a parakeet.
I like to talk
and chatter
like
    a
       parakeet.
— Marlene, age 10

David tells us this.

I'd like to be
a dog.
Ar-r-r-r-r-r-
-arr-r-r-r-r.
I will walk noisy.
I'll bark at people
and
BITE
them!
I will eat Terry dog food . . .
Yum-yum-yum-m-m . . .
I will look mean.
— David M., age 8

David took evident pleasure in putting together the letters
that would stand for the menacing growl of a dog. The
poem is interesting since David's good nature and
mild manner were famous in the third grade classroom that year. None of us knew that he wanted to be so
ferocious. Sometimes people discover things they didn't
know they knew about themselves when they begin to
write self-portraits.

Have you ever had the feelings Katie is describing
in this poem?

Sometimes
I feel like a turtle
walking on the sand
or a snail
inching along.
Sometimes
I feel so lazy
that I could just trip
over anything
that is before me.
It would be
so hard
     to
        pick
            up
               a
             pin.
— Katie, age 11

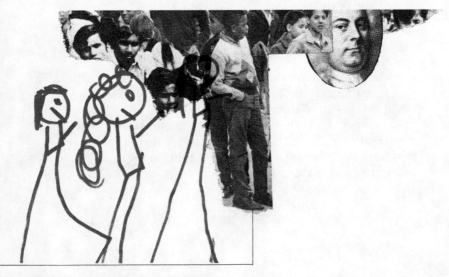

Another myself-as-a-turtle poem comes to us from Maria R. of Micronesia.

The Turtle
(A poem of myself)

A turtle that has been short of air
In the depth of the ocean,
Struggling madly,
Kicking against water,
Trying to come up
For another supply
Of oxygen.
But he can't
For one of his legs has been caught
By a giant clam
Far down the depth
Of the vast ocean.

— Maria R., age 17

It is a powerful poem, with strong words to show us the breathless, choking panic of the animal. The closing lines, "Far down the depth/Of the vast ocean," seem to pull us down, down with the turtle itself.

After your students have spent some time painting themselves with words, ask them to paint word pictures of their friends. When they have finished, ask for volunteers to read their word portraits to the class. Have the class guess who is being described.

Mitsuo S. was one of the members of the Micronesian class whose poems you have been reading. Two of his classmates used him as subject matter when they were asked to write a character study. What kind of picture do you see when you combine the two impressions of Mitsuo?

Mitsuo

Silence dwells in him always
but once a word parts the two attached lips,
you can hardly remain unlaughing.
Slowness is always maintained in his walk,
Kindness and generosity can be read clearly on
    the face,
Wherever this slim and slender clown walks,
There is apt to be laughter.

               — Maria R., age 17

And now, see him through different eyes.

      Slim, slender and tall like a mast of a
        schooner.
      And swaying side to side, back and forth as
M   he moves,
i   His aloha, waving smoothly as a sail
t   fastened to the mast.
s   His voice, deep and low, attracts the crew.
u He enjoys the happiness and the worth of
o   life,
      And in him there is no seriousness, almost,
      But the kind Nature has given him the spell
      To calm the fierce tiger,
      And alter the silence of the world.

               — Masaharu, age 19

The affectionate regard of Maria and of Masaharu for their classmate is obvious. These descriptions were so apt, as a matter of fact, that when the poems were originally read, without titles, the class had no hesitation in shouting, "Mitsuo!"

Mitsuo, too, wrote a character study. This one is untitled, but it is obviously a description of a strong, dominant man. In the last line, the word *you*, puts the reader directly in the path of this man.

> Come the typhoon, come the fire,
> What he says never changes.
> Roaring of electric power-plant,
> Noises created by the crowd of the whole world:
> People playing on the farthest end of the earth
> Have no difficulty hearing his voice when he talks.
> Tight . . . hard . . . twisted,
> He comes toward you with shadows of muscles.
> — Mitsuo, high school

When Ulai uses the word *queer* in the next poem, she means crazy, silly, or acting foolish.

M. Leerngof
Obese, bulgy, plump,
She is an elephant.
She is more queer than more serious.
When the world is in silence,
She can converse it into noisiness.
While she is serious, she causes laughter,
when she is queer, she causes seriousness.
But after the gleam of glee,
she is all discouraged and gloomy.
— Ulai, age 16

Kelly sums up her friend Charlene for us in just four lines.

Charlene
fearlessly laughing
she wraps the world in humor
and drops the pink-bowed thing
into her pocket.
— Kelly, high school

167   *People and More People*

Here is a cinquain, a character study in just five lines.

Laurie
has thumb in mouth
In a world of her own
Blaming people for her mistakes:
Laurie.

— Debbie, age 13

Writing a character study in cinquain has the same advantages that writing other cinquains on other subjects has. The restricted form forces the writer to look for exactly the right words, to focus in on specifics that present a succinct word portrait.

Here is Mary's portrait of her friend Ann.

Ann
A tuning fork of feathers
On which the slightest breeze
May play a single note
That rings, reverberates
and stings my face with tenderness.

(She loves her world away.)

Sudden!
Treftings crash
Apart and
Must be Puzzled together
Transcintly.

A tuning fork of feathers.

— Mary, age 16

Like the words in Lewis Carroll's "The Jabberwocky," *treftings* and *transcintly* are not part of our vocabularies. But, in Mary's study of Ann, we are able to read them with some understanding of their meaning. At least they don't get in the way of the essential picture of Ann as a "tuning fork of feathers."

168   *A Celebration of Bees*

Alison wrote about Jane one summer.

Jane's hair —
soft and wet.
Pearls of light raindrops
on each strand of hair
when she is walking
through the rain.
— Alison, age 11

Not a character study, really, but it is a skillful use of words by a young girl to describe her friend "when she is walking through the rain."

Not only our friends, but members of our own families can sit for their word portraits. Think about people who live in your house — the people you see most and, perhaps, know best. What words can you use to sum up your mother, your father, your brothers and sisters? Can you think of a single characteristic that defines each of your family members?

Many people have pet expressions that they say again and again. Some people use their hands in certain characteristic ways. We recognize some by their posture. These are the kinds of special *noticings* we can do when trying to realize a person's image accurately in words. Judge for yourself whether the essential inner qualities of Tosiwo's father come out in this next poem.

My Father

His words are sacred to me.
He shoots with love, but nobody can see it.
The earth is revolving,
but his words are straight as a sword to me.
People think he is only a man. However,
I consider him as the only man who has two
      hearts,
One for blood circulation, and one for love.
— Tosiwo Nakamura

Roxanne found many moods to speak of when she decided to describe her brother.

My Brother
My brother is like stones
Dropping on glass
When he is angry.
If he is mean like a whip,
He cuts.
He is like a piece
Of wood
Or a goofy clown
When he feels lazy,
Or like smooth fishes swimming.
When nice,
He is like a soft pillow
You rest your head on.
Asleep, he is like
soft droning
(Except, he SNORES!)
That is my brother:
Nice, kind, mean, angry
sleeping
and awake.

— Roxanne, high school

Here is Joe's cinquain portrait of his brother.

Brother:
Friend? Enemy?
Someone you can talk to.
Big and strong like a gorilla.
My friend.

— Joe, age 12

In her description of a child, Sylvia is looking back toward a time when she was small.

Towering dreamland,
Transcending dandylions,
I encircled all for my menagerie.
From tablespoon minnows
dressed in sequins
decorating my jovial creek
to my grass geysers
caressing my chocolated
earth cake,
All was mine,
crisp and free.
Now my record player
sings my tune.

— Sylvia, high school

Sylvia's extravagant language reminds me of "Fern Hill," a poem of childhood by Dylan Thomas whose use of words for their color, their sound, their shape on the tongue appeals to children as well as adults. Try listening with the children to the "Fern Hill" recording listed in the Bibliography. It has often served as a lively catalyst for poems.

Here is childhood, not remembered, but presently observed.

Head-of-curls
Slumbers.
Wind-Sunshine-Flowers-Birds
Pillowed in daylight post.
Chubby hand
Clutches
Silk-Softness-Friend-Blanket
As Teddy sentinels the crib.

— Peggy, high school

Older people lend themselves to character studies. Alison was only eleven when she imagined what it would be like to grow old.

> I rode horses,
>   no more.
> I laughed and sang
> with the other kids —
>   never again.
> I sat by the creek
>   and observed.
> Can I now?
>   No. I am old.

— Alison, age 11

Loneliness and wistfulness are quietly depicted for us in the following study of an elderly man. The author stays out of it, and we simply eavesdrop as the man speaks with a visitor.

Sit down and talk awhile. Isn't it a beautiful day? . . . Yes, it has been a nice year, but I have been lonely. You know my wife died last spring. She was a good wife and a good mother of our eight children . . . Yes, we had eight: five boys and three girls; but they have all grown up and have children of their own to care for. Sometimes they come to visit me, but I rarely see three of them because they live in other states . . . No, they keep suggesting that, too, but those old folks homes are for the people that are sick or alone and forgotten. And, after all, I do have eight children who come to see me, sometimes. . .

— Patty H., high school

The man's words, by themselves, paint us a portrait. Patty was able to "get inside the skin" of this man and speak with his voice.

Looking at photographs and paintings of people is another good way to motivate the writing of character studies. Julie, a sixth grader, wrote about Cezanne's painting, *Victor Chocquet.*

> Stern, but gentle. A man with a touch of a grin. Not a political man. But a log cabin man. He gets very vulgar at times. But other times wonderful words come from the mouth. He is not stunning in his old age, and he does not try to be Dashing to impress us.
> — Julie C., age 10

After studying the painting *Helle Babbe, Witch of Haarlem* by the Dutch painter Frans Hals, an eighth grade girl wrote this analysis of the strange-looking woman.

> She sits alone, hissing and cursing at other people. Her owl stands over her like the devil. Her face is aged with her problems and her meanness. When she smiles, all you see is black; teeth are gone. With her beery, winey breath she goes around sneaking behind other people's backs. But as the clock strikes the magical hour, she gets a certain wild and ferocious feeling growling in her. She cannot control her rage. It's boiling in her! She is going mad!
> — Debbie, age 13

Farmer's Wife by Grant Wood gave Jennifer her idea for a word portrait. The painting shows only an elderly lady, with a farm behind her, sitting and holding a sansevieria in a clay pot.

The Happy, Lonely Lady

Boiling, steaming sun staring me right in the eyes. I'm all alone. But I have lots of things that mean so much to me. I have my house and the plant that my husband planted for me before he died. This living plant will keep me living with pride.

— Jennifer, age 13

In the books we read, we come to know characters through the words authors use to describe them. When a writer tells us that an old lady "extends her claw" to pick up a little cake, we have an immediate reaction to her: she is not going to be a gentle, soft, loving character in the story.

Writers can give clues to peoples' characters and personalities just by describing their body movements. With this in mind, I asked the children to reach into the mystery box and choose a slip of paper from it. Each paper contained a short statement about a person. The children were to write a description showing us how this person moves about.

Julie's mystery slip said: "This fearful little person is afraid of everything." Julie's description tells us who this little person is.

A flittering little girl who is in the corner and hides every time someone passes. When walking, she slips on her heel or toe. She has her head in her arms, too!

— Julie, age 10

Jennifer, age twelve, created a character from the same mystery slip in just one short clause, ". . . and when I said 'hi' she shriveled up in a ball and started to cry."

Tina picked the mystery slip, "The General arrives."

The General arrives. He walks like an elephant and never is polite. His head swings like an elephant with a headache and he trumpets out orders.

— Tina, age 12

Tina's portrait is a fine example of the consistent use of a simile. The general does, indeed, seem "like an elephant," with head swinging (an excellent touch), and his orders trumpeted out.

George's mystery slip read, "A robber comes around the corner."

He slinks around the corner with the cunning of a snake ready to strike.

— George, age 12

Using the same mystery slip, Anne described a different thief.

The thief was slinking back into the dark, mysterious alley. You could faintly hear the clod of his feet as he stealthily crept away. He stumbled, staggered, and fell into the trap.

— Anne, age 12

Rita's slip of paper read, "The clowns are coming."
Her little piece begins with an -*ing* word that immediately
starts us off in the direction Rita wants us to go.

Jumping, twirling into the tent, making
funny and weird noises, the clowns came.
— Rita, age 10

Other mystery slips that day included these: "A
tired nurse tries to do her job." "A businesslike teacher
gets her room ready." "The bully comes out to the play-
ground." "The witch comes down the dark stairway."
"A farmer drives a load of hay home in the cool evening."
"A construction worker looks up in time to see a rope
break." "A fireman rushes to find equipment when the
alarm goes off."

Writers often choose names for their characters so
that we can see them more clearly. Charles Dickens
named a character Uriah Heep. That is a name that makes
us see — what? What kind of names would you give to a
town drunk, a college professor, a piano teacher, a pretty
teacher, a fat banker, and a poor old man?

Jennifer gave those characters these names:

college professor — Prof. Everett
pretty teacher — Mrs. Trotta
fat banker — Mr. Bergantail
poor old man — Mr. Nelson

And Tina's list was quite different, of course:

college professor — Prof. Willdle
piano teacher — Mrs. Dollarson
pretty teacher — Miss Kathy Bronson
fat banker — Harry Bette
poor old man — Charlie Wilson

In both lists there are some excellent names — names that make us see a person. Which teacher do you think is prettier, Mrs. Trotta or Miss Kathy Bronson? Which is the poorer old man, Mr. Nelson or Charlie Wilson? Of the two fat bankers which seems the fattest, Mr. Bergantail or Harry Bette? It's an interesting exercise and one that never fails to involve the children's imaginations.

You can also give a character's name and ask students to describe that person. For example, who is Henry Glockaspear? Marilyn was sure she knew him and described him this way.

> Henry Glockaspear is a middle-age square. He's really hung up on Bach, Beethoven, and Mozart. He has black hair with a grey streak. He wears spectacles that hang on the tip of his nose. His clothes are old-fashioned and he hates children very much.
>
> — Marilyn, age 13

Can you imagine someone who is named Mrs. Beulah Umpar? Jennifer can.

> . . . Delightful, nice old lady. Owns apartment house . . . grey hair . . . always laughing . . . she wears old fashion clothes, tries to understand the world . . . friends to everyone . . .
>
> — Jennifer, age 13

Thirteen-year-old Debbie sees a character named Sally Bladden as "ugly with warts (spoiled) . . . red hair . . . hazel eyes . . . a mean baby sitter . . . 13 years old."

Meet Miss Millie Pinter. What kind of person does your imagination show you? Notice the sounds in her name. How do they suggest a different character from the sounds that the name Beulah Umpar suggest? Is there such a thing as a heavy name? A lightweight name?

Miss Millie Pinter

Fluttering, continually fluttering . . .
Now flitting over to examine a flower.
Flying on feet
as light as feathers
Darting about
seeing and hearing . . .
Everything.
Similar to a chickadee:
never resting.

— Suebee, age 11

The name, Miss Millie Pinter, with its short *i* sounds reminded the young poet of light, quick actions and images. Wouldn't a character named Mrs. Beulah Umpar need an entirely different description? The sounds in her name are slow and heavy. Say them and see how they hit your ear and your imagination.

We have met many people on these pages. We have seen self-portraits in this gallery. We have seen portraits of friends and relatives. People have come to life because of words! Ideas can come from everywhere.

Use paintings, portraits and self-portraits, as I have suggested in this chapter. You can also use photographs from home, photos of children and elderly people, photos of crowds and close-ups of faces in crowds, photos of well-known people in a particular mood, photos from newspapers and magazines. Have your students write sketches like the ones in this chapter. Have them become the person in the picture as they write. Or they can be observers writing about the picture.

Pick names from literature that your students are not familiar with. Have them write descriptions of the characters who own those names. Then compare the children's descriptions with how the author originally conceived of the characters. Or have the children read descriptions of characters from literature and then name those characters. Then compare their names with the original names the author chose for the characters.

Write descriptions of TV characters in terms of the way the actors' movements and attitudes make us believe in their personalities. Imagine a TV character portrayed by a different actor. How would the new actor have to change his or her ways of walking, gesturing, speaking?

People and more people! Find them and show them to us. Words will be the brush, the camera, the tools to make us see — people.

Bibliography

Blackburn, Paul. "The Stone." In *Some Haystacks Don't Even Have Any Needle: And Other Complete Modern Poems*, edited by Stephen Dunning, Edward Lueders, Hugh Smith. Glenview, Ill.: Scott, Foresman and Company, 1969.

Coatsworth, Elizabeth. "Asleep." In *The Sparrow Bush*. New York: Grosset and Dunlap, Inc., n.d.

Hitomaro. "A Strange Old Man." In *One Hundred Poems from the Japanese*, translated by Kenneth Rexroth. New York: New Directions Publishing Corp., 1955.

Holman, Felice. "When I'm Me," "The Child Who Cried," "Way Out There," "The Flower Trap." In *I Hear You Smiling*. New York: Charles Scribner's Sons, 1973.

Jordan, June. *Who Look at Me*. New York: Thomas Y. Crowell Company, 1969.

Lewis, Richard, ed. "People." In *Miracles: Poems by Children of the English-Speaking World*, pp. 133-150. New York: Simon and Schuster, Inc., 1966.

Masters, Edgar Lee. *Spoon River Anthology*. New York: The Macmillan Company, 1962.

Robinson, Edwin Arlington. "Richard Cory," "Miniver Cheevy," "Cliff Klingenhagen," "Flammonde," "Luke Havergoll." In *The Collected Poems*. New York: The Macmillan Company, 1937.

Sakanoe, Lady Otomo No. "You Say I Will Come." In *One Hundred Poems from the Japanese*, translated by Kenneth Rexroth. New York: New Directions Publishing Corp., 1955.

Sandburg, Carl. "Jazz Fantasia." In *Modern American Poetry*, edited by Louis Untermeyer. rev. ed. New York: Harcourt Brace Jovanovich, Inc., 1962.

_____. "My People," "Portrait of a Child Settling Down for an Afternoon Nap," "Hits and Runs," "Mother and Child," "Under a Hat Brim," "Sweeping Wendy." In *Wind Song*. New York: Harcourt Brace Jovanovich, Inc., 1960.

Teasdale, Sara. "The Crystal Gazer." In *Collected Poems of Sara Teasdale*, edited by Marya Zaturenska. New York: The Macmillan Company, 1953.

Thomas, Dylan. *A Child's Christmas in Wales*. New York: New Directions Publishing Corp., 1959.

––––––. "Fern Hill." In *Golden Journey: Poems for Young People*, edited by Louise Bogan and William J. Smith. Chicago: Reilly and Lee Company, 1965.

Whitman, Ruth. "Bicycling Downhill." In *The Marriage Wig and Other Poems*. New York: Harcourt Brace Jovanovich, Inc., 1966.

Williams, William Carlos. "This Is Just To Say." In *The Golden Journey: Poems for Young People*, edited by Louise Bogan and William J. Smith. Chicago: Reilly and Lee Company, 1965.

Wolfe, Humbert. "The Old Lady." In *This Singing World: Junior Edition*, edited by Louis Untermeyer. New York: Harcourt Brace Jovanovich, Inc., 1926.

Recording

"Fern Hill" in *Dylan Thomas Readings Vol. 1*. Caedmon record (TC 1002).

Animal Fair

"I went to the Animal Fair," starts an old rhyme by an unknown author, "and the birds and the beasts were there . . ." The birds and the beasts are here, too — in a whole chapter of word pictures done by children and young people.

In the last chapter we explored writing about people, all kinds and varieties of people. We noted that in describing a person, attitudes, gestures, speech patterns, a variety in clothing, names, and other attributes distinguish one person from others.

But describing an animal can become more difficult. We need to think carefully about each word that will help the reader see our animals better. We need to search out colorful words that will let the reader feel the massive weight and sway of an elephant, the lightness and bounce of a kitten, an alley cat's prowl, the soar and drop of a fish hawk. We need also to search for words to distinguish one elephant from another. We need to look for a way to tell our readers that we are describing one particular kitten, rather than all kittens. All of these creatures differ from one another, and the writer must work skillfully to show these differences.

Let's talk about the ways in which poets decide just what word is most appropriate for their special needs. If we are describing a tiny animal that moves quickly, we need to look for words that move quickly too. We've already mentioned the relative speeds of words, how the sound of the word we use can suggest the meaning we want to convey. The word *quick* has a short *i* sound followed by a staccato consonant sound; it moves rapidly as we say it. On the other hand, the word *slow* sounds and moves much less rapidly because of the long vowel sound.

Fill the chalkboard with a snowstorm of animal-movement words. Ask your students how tiny animals move. What do they look like? Ask for fast, tiny-sounding words like *skitter* and *scurry*. How many words can they think of that mean the same as running fast and lightly? How does an elephant move? An ox? Ask for heavy words like *lumbering* and *wallow* and *stomp*. How does a leopard move? Ask for powerful-sounding words like *pounce, swoop, thrust,* or *spring*.

You might call out the names of animals, birds, insects, sea creatures and let the children provide words for each one until the board is filled and the word supply is exhausted. Use a book which describes all kinds of animals from the most familiar to the most exotic. If no one knows exactly what a certain animal is like, show a picture of it and give the pertinent facts: where it lives, what it eats, how it defends itself. It's fun to introduce yourself to a new animal by trying to find the exact words to describe it. When you've finished, you will have a menagerie of words to start ideas exploding into lively writing.

Coleen thought about a swan, concentrated on all of the most swan-like characteristics she could call to mind, and came up with a piece of writing that seemed to her classmates to be an accurate, imaginative picture. Do you agree?

Swan

The swan thrashed her webbed pads behind her in the swirling water. She went gliding across the lake like a leaf glides to the ground in a soft wind.

Then, she waddled onto the shore and across the waving grass. Then, turning around, she swept back to the shore and the swirling water, where the swan again floated in peace on the lake.

— Coleen, age 15

Is *thrashed* a good choice for the action of the swan's feet? Do you like "webbed pads" better than "webbed feet"? Is the comparison between the swan's glide and a leaf's glide a good one? Do you like the contrast between the gliding swan in the water and the waddling swan on the shore? How would you write a piece about a swan?

Feather Tree
Shimmer,
the water reflects
ringlets of light
onto the feathery tree
on the shore.
One brown duck
swims under the tree.
Smoothly gliding along,
she joins
the rest of the ducks.

— Jane E., age 11

Jane's primary interest — her motivation for writing — was the play of light on a narrow-leafed mountain ash in the fall. The slim leaves of mountain ash are arranged along a central stem, and each branch does seem to be made of feathers. The image "ringlets of light" shows an intuitive sense of language, used with grace and ease.

If you have ever watched a heron standing absolutely motionless in the water, waiting for a fish, you will appreciate the power of the image in the next poem.

Heron

A statue stands motionless on knobby stilts.
Nothing stirs but her plumage startled by the
    wind.
Slowly, slowly one eye opens —
Then a steely needle flashes, burning the water.
Silence returns without a sound to hurt it.
A statue stands motionless on knobbly stilts . . .

— Mary C., high school

Mary has obviously observed this bird with great interest, and her picture is stunning in its accuracy. The piece begins with all movement suspended. Only plumage "stirs . . . startled by the wind ." And then, with the slow opening of an eye, *all* is movement — the beak that "flashes" into the water, the splash we can almost hear and see in our minds as bird stabs fish. The circular form of the whole piece, with the last line repeating the first line exactly, returns us to the vigil of the heron. The ellipsis at the end of the last line was placed there by the poet to show us that it will all begin again.

Anne sees small, brown sparrows in a group that seem to be conversing.

Sparrows

Sparrows sit on the windowsill
gossiping
'til their heads
fall off.

— Anne, age 11

The Bird

Time is irrelevant to
    my blazing, yellow and
    boisterous
       clock.

He sings his song
    to the day,
caring not — what
    I say.

— Mary M., high school

We don't know exactly what kind of bird we see here,
but we have a clue that tells us he is a true early bird.

Eagles are, understandably, a favorite subject for
writers. When Joseph actually saw an eagle high in a
northern Minnesota sky, he wrote a spur-of-the-moment
poem.

I saw an eagle in the sky
flying so free and high.
I wish I could join him
in his dance
in the sky.

— Joseph, age 13

When he brought it to the group and read it aloud,
there were some carefully considered criticisms from the
other youngsters. And Joseph had to rethink his work.

187 *Animal Fair*

Everyone agreed that "his dance in the sky" was an unusual and fitting way to describe the bird's flight. They were bothered by "so free and high," since the word, *so* does nothing but weaken the expansive feeling of "free and high." *So* can be used successfully to mean *very* only when it is followed by an example. For example, "It is so cold outside," does not express the extent of coldness as well as, "It is so cold outside that my breath froze on my eyelashes." In the second sentence, *so* becomes a good tool to tell us exactly how cold, hot, or whatever.

The children also thought, after hearing Joseph read his poem several more times, that "in the sky" in line one was not necessary. They agreed that *high* tells us that the eagle is "in the sky." It turned out, then, that Joseph only had to remove four words! But see how taut and strong his poem becomes with those four words taken out.

> I saw an eagle
> flying free and high.
> I wish I could join him
> in his dance in the sky.
> — Joseph, age 13

Another eagle appears in this little scene.

> The eagle peers down from its high perch looking for a meal, then swoops down quietly and swiftly and clutches its prey.
> — Emily, age 10

Emily's choice of words shows her concern for strong images: *peers, swoops, quietly, swiftly,* and *clutches.* These are eagle words.

Look for the descriptive words in this following piece of writing. Can you see the lion, see the flash of light, feel the bullet?

Hunting Safari

At the deepness of the night an old lazy lion curls up. He just settles down and smells something. It goes away . . . and comes again . . . now! It's close! Jumping up, he rushes into a fury of light. Stunned by brightness, he roars. A sharp, stone-like thing hits him! The dark, spooky shadows roam around him . . . He wakes up in the Happy Hunting Ground.

— Anne, age 11

Anne's use of phrases like "stunned by brightness" and "a fury of light" shows us her unusually perceptive ear and a real awareness of the power of the words she chooses. Look at her out-of-the-ordinary "shadows roam." If you will say this phrase aloud several times you will see that it has a low, dark sound appropriate to the description of a dying animal. You'd have a hard time saying "shadows roam" in a quick, lighthearted way, or in a high-pitched voice. Try it.

You can appreciate Anne's eleven-year-old expertise when you realize how *right* her choice of language is in this short piece. To see what it is we mean by writing creatively, explore Anne's poem and other poems carefully, word by word, with your students.

189 *Animal Fair*

Steven writes about deer. Then he adds wolves, and ends with the most powerful wolf words he could think of.

Out in the Forest
Snow falling gently
The wind blowing
in the forest,
the deer running swift.
The wolves attacking
the deer —
The deer leaps over
and into the brush.
The deer runs
fast as it can
from
the scissor jaws.

— Steven, age 10

Earlier, you met Emily's swooping eagle. Here is her cat.

The cat creeps along lightly and swiftly on its delicate paws, ready to pounce on a mouse.

— Emily, age 10

And here is a mouse.

Ebony streak slinks by —
Luminous eyes search —
Bits of light —
Now she stops —
Crouched, Tense.
Waiting.

— Debby, high school

A giraffe stops to have its portrait drawn for us,
thanks to Peggy's inner vision and ability to use language
in new ways.

Giraffe

A brown and gold lattice piece
    summits
    the sky.
The legs
    on four stilts —
    the expanse of earth.
She tongues the leafy growth
    Vaulting
    Racing
    Speeding
    across the savannah.

— Peggy, high school

Look at Peggy's giraffe once again and see the accuracy of the image "brown and gold lattice piece." The word *summits* is another example of a verb made from a word generally used as a noun. *Stilts* has been used twice in this chapter about animal descriptions — first for the heron's legs and now for the giraffe's. Is it an appropriate word in both instances? Is it more suitable and exact in one poem than in the other? Can you improve upon the word in either poem? How? Experiment and see what you can do.

Listen to the sound *umb* in many of the words in the next poem and ask if the repetition of that sound adds to our sense of the characteristics of polar bears. How does it do this? Use the chalkboard to write some more polar bear words.

Polar bears tumble
with a scurry rumble
right into a puddle
while they're in deep slumber
on a winter's morn.

— Ruth, high school

Connie's poems tend to rhyme, and she uses rhyming words in an easy, natural way. This poem has a feeling of stopped action, like a movie of horses suddenly stopped short and held as a still-picture for us to see.

Dry Summer Evening
Chestnuts, roans, a black, a bay,
Scattered in the deep dark way.
Heavy hearts because of thirst,
with jagged wounds that should be nursed.
A stallion so willing to fight for his herd,
The watchful lead mare awaiting the word.

— Connie, age 10

This poem is from one of the young writers in Micronesia.

Octopus

Sitting on a coral like a coral
Resting on the sand like the sand
With his eight arms spreading out
He catches with stride his food.

The king of all the sea creatures
Soft and flexible body without bones
Yet kills even the giant whale
With his black smoky weapon
And hundreds of suckers on his arms.

But he's afraid of the heavenly phenomena
For when the lightning flashes across the sky
He shall flee and vanish under the coral
And when the thunder roars over him
He holds the coral and shrinks himself.

Each time the thunder rolls and roars
He will break his arms one by one
And when the hunger strikes him at once
He eats his broken arms greedily.

When the thunder is gone and the sky is clear
He sits again on a coral like a coral
With his eight broken arms spreading out
And still he is the king of the sea.

— Masaharu, age 20

Now you've met all the animals in this poetic carnival, this parade of birds and beasts from the Animal Fair as seen by young writers from many places. The common thread that binds all of this writing into a single piece is the poets' interest in words and their power to perform on the page. This willingness to experiment, to

sample many words before choosing the best one for the
job, is a satisfying result of the no-holds-barred attitude
toward language that these young people accepted with
enthusiasm and delight.

Bibliography

Cole, William, ed. *The Birds and the Beasts Were There.*
New York: World Publishing Co., 1963.

Conkling, Hilda. "Red Rooster," "Chickadee." In
This Singing World: Junior Edition, edited by Louis
Untermeyer. New York: Harcourt Brace Jovanovich,
Inc., 1926.

Deutsch, Babette. "Ape." In *Some Haystacks Don't Even
Have Any Needle: And Other Complete Modern Poems,*
edited by Stephen Dunning, Edward Lueders,
Hugh Smith. Glenview, Ill.: Scott, Foresman and
Company, 1969.

Dickinson, Emily. "A bird came down the walk," "A
narrow fellow in the grass." In *Selected Poems and
Letters of Emily Dickinson,* edited by Robert Linscott.
Garden City, N. Y.: Doubleday & Company, Inc.,
Anchor Books, 1959.

Esbensen, Barbara J. "Robin." In *Swing Around the Sun.*
Minneapolis, Minn.: Lerner Publications Co., 1965.

Lewis, Richard, ed. "Creatures." In *Miracles: Poems by
Children of the English-Speaking World,* pp. 85-102.
New York: Simon and Schuster, Inc., 1966.

Sandburg, Carl. "Bluebird, What Do You Feed On?"
"Goldwing Moth." In *Wind Song.* New York: Harcourt Brace Jovanovich, Inc., 1960.

Sexton, Anne. "Torn Down from Glory Daily." In
The Wind Is Round, edited by Sara Hannum and
John T. Chase. New York: Atheneum Publishers,
1970.

Stevens, Wallace. "13 Ways of Looking at a Black-
bird." In *Collected Poems.* New York: Alfred A.
Knopf, 1954.

Swenson, May. "News from the Cabin." In *A Cage of Spines*. New York: Rinehart and Company, 1958.

_____. "Cat and the Weather." In *The Wind Is Round*, edited by Sara Hannum and John T. Chase. New York: Atheneum Publishers, 1970.

Walker, Ted. "The Harpooning." In *The Wind Is Round*, edited by Sara Hannum and John T. Chase. New York: Atheneum Publishers, 1970.

Animating the Inanimate

In the two previous chapters, we have seen that words, used with imagination and skill, can bring to three-dimensional life people, animals, birds, and insects of all kinds. We can show the inner feelings of a person simply by describing a walk, or the tilt of a head; we can give ferocity to a lion, flight to a dragonfly, or lanky-legged height to a giraffe.

All this is accomplished by merely choosing the right words. By this time, it must be evident that words are magical and powerful. We can use them to do our bidding. We can be as powerful ourselves as any wizard!

Writers often write about nonliving, inanimate things as though those things were alive. The American writer, Willa Cather, in her novel *O Pioneers*, described old pioneer houses on the prairie as though they were animals — cattle, perhaps.

> The dwelling houses were set about haphazard on the tough prairie sod; some of them looked as if they had been moved in overnight, and others as *if they were straying off by themselves, headed straight for the open prairie.*

It is hard to think of a more effective way to show the reader that small, impermanent Nebraska town than to say the houses looked as though they'd been "moved in overnight" and that some others seemed to be "straying off by themselves. . ." like dumb animals on the prairie.

In "The Clock," we see an inanimate object described as an old man.

The Clock

An old man sits.
Your hands used to go
so fast.
Now they shake
and go
so slowly.

— Rita, age 10

Here is another old man. This time we see him in wintry branches stretched against the cold sky.

Branches

Cold, stiff —
like an old man stretching his arms,
trying to get the bitter frost
out of his body.

— Debbie, age 13

How can you motivate children to look at an inanimate object and see it as something with a life of its own — breathing and alive?

As an example, think of automobiles. What can they remind us of? Put the word *automobiles* on the chalkboard. What living things come to mind when we think of automobiles? Animals? What are the animals doing? Do they eat? How? Do they make sounds? What sounds? List as many as you can. Why are these creatures making the sounds? Do they think? What are they thinking? Why? Are there family groups of automobiles? Here is a possible list of words for your chalkboard: *whine, nuzzle, bucking, sleek, blinking, starting, stray, nosing, tracks, crouch, spring, delicate, race, strong.* How can we use these words to describe our animal-automobiles?

Think about a long line of trucks moving along. Here is Debbie's word picture. She uses two animal images to describe her trucks. Is one better than the other? Why? With what animal would you compare this line of trucks?

> Truck convoy: like ants following each other, carrying their food home. Or, like elephants moving along slowly, stomping and telling everything in their way to move.
>
> — Debbie, age 13

Think of a highway full of cars at night. Are the headlights eyes? Whose eyes are they? Where do they go? Why do they stop? What do they see? Do they blink? Sally can see them clearly in her imagination.

Cars at Night
Released from their cages
into a dark . . .
blinking their eyes,
skidding around a corner they go,
bracing the road.

— Sally A., age 13

Proof that we think of cars as animals can be seen in the names manufacturers give them. By naming a car Jaguar the company presents us with an untamable wildcat, not a mere steel body and engine! Maverick, Mustang, and Pinto all immediately give their characteristics to the vehicle. We aren't buying just wheels and chassis — we are buying strength and speed and flying manes. We are even buying the idea of speed-as-flight when we choose our Falcon, our Firebird, our Thunderbird! And if we want ferocity, we can choose a Cougar or a Barracuda. One company has a small car that it calls a Cricket. How does this car behave? What are its characteristics? How would you describe it in an advertisement?

Put a list of *things* on the chalkboard and ask the students to choose one or more that appeals to them.

For each one chosen, ask the students to make it live, first, by giving it human characteristics, and second, animal traits. Your list could include these things and more: old shoes, clock, house, skyscraper, mobile home park, rocks, mountains, scissors, clothes on hangers, clothing on a floor, gloves, mittens, numbers, letters of the alphabet.

Along with a list, you might put names of things on slips of paper to be picked out, one at a time, from the mystery box that we've mentioned in these chapters.

Or have a tableful of actual objects for animating from which interested students can choose. Actually seeing an old boot, an antique satin slipper, a worn pocket watch or a delicate wristwatch might trigger responses which merely naming that object could not accomplish.

Photographs, too, offer a wide range of possibilities. A picture of eggs in a carton might result in an amusing image. A chair tilted back against a porch wall, a lumpy jacket draped over a railing, a spritely sailboat slanted against the waves — all these pictures could be idea starters.

Once you begin to think about how you would animate something, the pictures you seek out in magazines and newspapers will find you. You will note possibilities in every photo you see. You might find lines of telephone poles or mounds of grapefruit or oranges in the food advertisements. When you see a picture of twigs, snow covered bushes huddled on the lawn, or a cluster of flowers nodding in the wind, you'll think, "Why, yes, they could be . . . ." Start thinking about animation, and your picture collection will grow apace. The students can bring pictures for the gallery of inanimates, as well, and there'll be no stopping the flow of images these pictures will generate.

As a matter of fact, you and your students may find that after playing with animating the inanimate for a while, it will be hard to shake the habit. You will begin to see a personality in every chair you see. (Look! It has knees! Elbows! A lap!) No tool on your garage shelf or cabbage in your garden will remain inanimate.

No soup tureen or soup pot or sugar bowl and lid will ever be content to sit placidly on your kitchen shelf again. Instead, you'll see them as a fat family. The tureen has her hands on her hips, her hair in a bun atop her head; the soup pot, with its big belly and one arm pointing severely, scowls at you now; and the little round sugar bowl folds its fat arms and wishes it could keep its domed hat from sitting askew.

Or, look at a sugar bowl in a totally different way, as Pattie did.

A bird lands
in the kitchen cupboard,
sitting there
with its wings straight,
big
    belly
        full.
                — Pattie, age 10

I hope you are willing to risk being haunted by your own possessions. The life with which you and your students imbue these objects is bound to delight you every time. What do you see when you read this poem?

Gleaming eyes
big and black,
following me
from side to side.
Two chimneys
for two ears up high.
A door for his nose.
Sad and lonely in despair —
Poor old house
on a hillside.
                — Dorothy K., age 8

Natural phenomena can be animated with great success. Some sort of animal with a huge mouth and claws is being described in this next poem. What do you see?

Today,
Nature swallowed
the sun.
The shore was clawed
with
the prey-seeking
waters.

— Nancy, high school

These animals are also frantic to get to the shore.

The rusty tiger-waves pounce to the shore.
Caring for none but themselves,
they leap on each other's backs
trying to get to their prey
where they will gorge themselves
on the sand
and roll back,
satisfied.

— Pat, high school

Marilyn writes about the same waves-meet-shore scene, but she sees it altogether differently. Does her image surprise you?

Waves,
like old ladies in white hats
coming home
to the shore —
noisily whispering about . . .
. . . something . . .
what, I don't know.

— Marilyn, age 13

From a Micronesian girl, we have the tigers again.

The Sea

You're calm and peaceful when the world is
     silent,
But you're fierce and wild like a wild tiger
When the wind comes from the East,
So fierce like you.
The sky turns to grey, but you
     will turn to white,
Because you're crushing reefs, shores, rocks.
Be calm always,
Because your beauty depends upon your calm-
     ness.

— Dengelei, high school

Another Micronesian student names the wind *King*
in this poem.

Wind, King of Nature

You!!! Who are you?!
Where are you from, You —?
As I gaze at the grass on the hillside
I see you're at work, at your everlasting job.
You send green waves upward the mountain,
One after the other;

You make trees handsome and beautiful,
Like young men and women
With their hair tossed backward.

You make the beautiful blue ocean
Even more beautiful.
You create surfs and break them again,
Causing white parts in the vast ocean of blue,
Creating a terrific scene of blue and white.

Up in the sky,
You rule over the ocean of clouds.
You send them over the world with your order
Of where and when to spray
Your plantation of green.

Ah, you!
You crawl over me!
You're so gentle and caressing.

Where do you come from,
O King of Nature?!

— Maria, high school

The sun in this next poem is seen as a creature who
is a bit too noisy. Notice that the clouds, too, are made

to seem alive through the skillful use of two words —
wordless and *scatter*.

> Fresh white clouds
> gather together
> in wordless company
> to meet the rising sun,
> then quickly scatter
> before its boisterous greetings.
>
> — Kathy, high school

In this poem, a cinquain, we see the sun in a new
role.

The Sun as Band Leader
> Rising,
> When you direct,
> Clish-clang goes the cymbals!
> You always get a headache
> but you don't mind —
> Good-day!
>
> — Tina, age 12

Judy gives us a breeze that can whistle and skate.
Can you see this breezy whistler?

> The whistling breeze
> Skated across the ocean
> Splashing long, whispering sprays
> Upon the shiny pebbles . . .
>
> — Judy O., high school

In her descriptive piece, Anne wants us to see, not only a quick glimpse of a real deer, but the breeze, too, as a running deer.

> Everything is motionless. The sounds of the forest drift away into the stillness. Suddenly, a deer bounds across the path and fades off into the never-ending woods. A cool, misty breeze blows by, as if it were being chased by hunters. The forest is then left with silence as a bird sings softly every now and then.
>
> — Anne L., age 11

Jennifer tries to understand rain talk in her poem.

Rain Drops
Who's dripping at my window?
What are you trying to say?
You're talking too fast.
Slow down. . .
— Jennifer, age 13

Tina writes:

Night,
in her black and white dress.
She only sees dark colors. . .
— Tina, age 10

A unique way of looking at spring occurred to Sally, when she studied the list of spring words on our chalkboard. The usual ideas were there, including *birds, nesting, rebirth, eggs, warmth.*

Spring,
imprisoned
by winter's crystallized egg,
pecks her way out
to a season
of love.

— Sally A., age 13

Sally took the images of rebirth and eggs and fashioned
a word picture for us that shows winter as a crystal
egg, with spring, an energetic fledgling, pecking and
chipping its way out of the confines of the cold season.

You can see from the poems and images written
here by children from fifth through twelfth grade that just
about any inanimate thing can be made to seem alive,
with either human or animal characteristics.

A group of children did just that, animating nu-
merals from one to ten after thinking hard about their
shapes and possible personalities. I asked them questions like these to help us see the number creatures:
How does the number stand? Or is it sitting down?
What other things are shaped like this particular number?
Does it remind you of a person? An animal? A bird?
Here are the results of this new way to see a group of
very familiar shapes.

1 is proud
because he just got
new cowboy boots
and a jacket
with stars on it,
1 is!

— Jane, age 8

2 is a jockey
that bounces on a horse
towards the end
of the track,
fighting
to be first.

— Pattie, age 10

3 is like hips,
knees, eyes. . .
sitting around the fire
roasting marshmallows on the fire. . .
Seagull.

— Tom G., age 10

4 is someone
trying to relax in the sun,
making a 4
with their legs
and lounging.

— Pattie, age 10

5,
nifty, nosey neighbors —
half-circle, other square —
running sleepwalker,
upside-down 2.

— Sue, age 12

6 is a flower bud
6 is a rocking-chair
6 is a person curling up
6 is!

— Caroline L., age 10

7 —
upside-down L,
ballerina's legs,
television antennas and
angles.
                          — Sue, age 12

8 —
Someone wearing glasses,
a small scribble design.
8 is a snowman,
bright, proud, happy.
                          — Caroline, age 10

9
is an upside-down 6.
He is a balloon
standing on a stick with one foot
9 is!
                          — Jane, age 8

10 is
an egg cracker
floating in the air
with a parachute on its back.
Ten was!
                          — Tom G., age 10

There are many ways to look at anything, as we
have repeatedly seen. Two children look at Time. One

sees it as a clock rushing us on; one sees it quite differently.

Time
Who's creeping around the clock so rapidly?
Where are you going? Who are you? Round and
round again. Every move you make screaming
and scolding, "Rush! Rush! Hurry!" STOP!
— Jennifer, age 13

For Jennifer, Time is a nagging nuisance, making us
tired, pushing us to do things faster and faster. Is this
the way Time appears to you? When do you get this
pressed feeling about Time?

In this next description we see a different picture
of Time.

Mr. Time
Why,
Mr. Time,
do you creep around
like a man walking
along,
Walking
so very slowly
down the lane?
— Joseph, age 13

Throughout this book we have discussed animation.
In various chapters I have suggested that you look at a
given thing — rain, wind, summer, the sea — as though
it were a man, a woman, an animal. But, in this chapter,
I hope you have seen the broader range of possibilities for creating some surprising and satisfying images
from some of the ordinary things we see every day.

Bibliography

Adams, Leonie. "Homecoming." In *This Singing World: Junior Edition*, edited by Louis Untermeyer. New York: Harcourt Brace Jovanovich, Inc., 1926.

Behn, Harry. "Lost," "Santa Fe West," "Thunder Dragon." In *The Golden Hive*. New York: Harcourt Brace Jovanovich, Inc., 1966.

Bennett, Rowena B. "Motor Cars." In *Piper, Pipe That Song Again*, edited by Nancy Larrick. New York: Random House, Inc., 1965.

Conkling, Hilda. "Dandelion." In *This Singing World: Junior Edition*, edited by Louis Untermeyer. New York: Harcourt Brace Jovanovich, Inc., 1926.

Dickinson, Emily. "I started early, took my dog." In *Selected Poems and Letters of Emily Dickinson*, edited by Robert Linscott. Garden City, N. Y.: Doubleday & Company, Inc., Anchor Books, 1959.

Hoban, Russell. "School Buses," "Typo." In *The Pedaling Man and Other Poems*. New York: Grosset and Dunlap, Inc., 1968.

Rich, Adrienne. "The Trees." In *The Wind Is Round*, edited by Sara Hannum and John T. Chase. New York: Atheneum Publishers, 1970.

Sandburg, Carl. "Four Preludes on Playthings of the Wind." In *Modern American Poetry*, edited by Louis Untermeyer. rev. ed. New York: Harcourt Brace Jovanovich, Inc., 1962.

_____. "Arithmetic," "Fourth of July Night," "Bubbles," "The Child Margaret," "Paper II." In *Wind Song*. New York: Harcourt Brace Jovanovich, Inc., 1960.

Swenson, May. "The Blindman," "The Even Lea." In *A Cage of Spines*. New York: Rinehart and Company, 1958.

Van Doren, Mark. "The Fields of November." In *The Wind Is Round*, edited by Sara Hannum and John T. Chase. New York: Atheneum Publishers, 1970.

Our Inner Spaces: Moods and Emotions

We have seen that poetry can be the expression of a personal response to any kind of experience. We have still to explore poetry writing as a response to our own inner selves. Feelings which are not usually shared daily with other people are often the subject and theme for poets.

In this chapter, you will find mostly examples by students of fourteen and older and fewer by young children. In some third grade groups, I did ask for expressions of feelings. But the results were generally ordinary and rather bland, with the exception of one or two examples included here. I think this sort of self-searching can be best accomplished by ninth graders, although you may want to try it with seventh or eighth graders. You can certainly experiment with it in the upper elementary grades, too, perhaps with quite good results.

But, it has been my experience that the older students do want to write about emotions and feeling moods. Uppermost in the teenagers' world are their emotions and growing self-awareness — their self-consciousness. Expression of these sometimes overpowering feelings will flow steadily upon the page once you provide the impetus.

The poems here deal with joy, fear, loneliness, old age, waiting, life, and death. There are none about love, although this is the age-old subject for poets. And I have no examples of poems about hate, either, although this, too, could bring out some interesting writing if you'd explore its possibilities with your students. The last section of the chapter explores ways poets can express many moods, emotions, and feelings through the use of color.

Let's see how many ways there are to think about joy. Are there some words that seem more joyful than others? What are they? Are there some special sounds you associate with feelings of happiness? Do you associate some colors with joy? What are some joyful ways to move? What is the taste of joy?

Listen to third graders as they tell of joy. In the first poem, Helen has used *swinging* and *dancing* to show her feelings.

Swinging along
on the nice breeze,
over the hill
and over the leaves
and dancing
on the big, bright, seas.

— Helen, age 8

Crystall, another third grader, writes:

Joy makes people happy
and it makes people
dance in the street.

— Crystall, age 8

In the next poem, we can see, taste, and feel one child's ideas of joy.

Joy
The colors of joy
are
Red, Purple, Pink.
The taste of joy
is
Turkey, chicken, and ham.
And the feel of joy
is
Fur, soap, and blankets.
— Lori, age 8

I've not, however, encouraged the kind of facile listing that abounds these days in the "unfinished sentence" (Happiness is . . ., etc.) sort of exercise. The serious searching-out of the right word, the strongest, clearest image, tends to be bypassed if you simply ask for lists. When facilitating creative writing, it's that word *creative* that is the most important one to focus upon.

In this unusual poem, another third grader makes a delightful comparison in the last line.

Lava is like water
running down a hill.
A light is like the sun
in the sky.
And a book is like a door
to joy.
— David, age 9

Do gold and silver remind you of joyous happen-

ings? Those colors turn up in both of the following poems.
First, one by a third grade girl:

> You can hear the band
> and horns playing.
> You can see the elephants
> marching
> with gold and silver blankets
> over their backs.
> See the soldiers playing drums!
> And look at all the people
> with gay and happy faces.
>
> — Delayne, age 8

And next, a poem written by one of the Micronesian
girls:

> A sunny day,
> with no gray clouds . . .
> A sun shines
> with its golden light,
> without any meaning,
> but bright,
> like a heart shining,
> swaying back and forth,
> beating like a watch
> on a wrist,
> and leaking
> with gold and silver.
>
> — Osiaol, age 17

Two poets, from opposite ends of the earth and of
different ages, use the idea of floating, of flying, with

joy. They describe the essence of joy as a singing bird.

        . . . You are happy.
        You feel like you are floating
        like a bird
        and singing . . .
                    — Tim, age 8

        The earth becomes a pebble
        and the sea
        a water-drop.
        All my past memories
        and hopes
        are painted gold.
        My mind wanders
        and my heart
        is like a singing bird . . .
        I feel my soul flying
        through the sea
        and my body sailing
        through the air;
        yet, the end is so quick
        leaving my heart
        hungry
        for the unreturning
        joy.
                    — Masaharu, age 19

Now that the United States' involvement in Viet-
nam has drawn to a stumbling close, a whole generation
of young people can live without its shadow on their

daily lives. Cynthia's curt understatement is included here as a war poem.

> Violence
> and war
> are a waste of time:
> ours
>   and
>   theirs.
>
> — Cynthia K., age 12

Cynthia tells us war is a waste of time. Is waiting also a waste of time? Read these next poems and see what you think.

Here are two Micronesian students' poetic expressions of the chore of waiting. They are giving us their feelings about the unending tedium, the frustrating, annoying, tiresome business of counting the minutes, hours, days . . . waiting.

> Standing for a second
> seems sitting for a minute;
> leaning for an hour
> means lying for a day
> and waiting for months
> seems expecting for years.
>
> Now the time and space
> seem eternal and unlimited:
> the ending seems
> still the beginning
> of waiting.
>
> Days and nights
> I swim
> against the coarse earth
> toward the unapproaching rim

of Heaven —
the horizon.

— Masaharu, age 20

Read the poem again, aloud, and see how the rhythm expresses the writer's hypnotic, suspended state. Have you ever had the slow motion, frustrated feeling that you are swimming "against the coarse earth . . ."?

This next poem is a similar expression of waiting.

Waiting.
Hour after hours —
waiting.
Nothing will be done
but waiting,
as an extreme punishment.
Waiting for a person,
I will not walk away
to comfort
my tiredness of waiting.
For if I walk away,
the person might come
that I may not be there
waiting.
So I stay,
waiting,
and waiting.
Waiting is tiresome work.

— Ulai, age 17

Loneliness is familiar to most people, and it's an easy feeling for young people to imagine, even if they have not yet experienced it themselves. A high school student once said to me, "I just think of all the things and people I love and need and then imagine my world without them, and I know how loneliness would be."

In her poem, Kathleen imagines herself to be a small
boy left to wait for someone, in the middle of a city,
on a bench.

Little Boy Lonely
I sit on my tiny bench,
alone in the world;
the people bustle by me
and there is no sympathy
or love
in their eyes.
The buildings,
tall and foreboding,
tower
over me
like cruel giants.

I am lonely
and forgotten.
The workmen
are getting out now.
Their cars speed by me —
Screeching
and growling,
like animals
in the jungle.

I am lonely
and forgotten.

— Kathleen, high school

Notice her imaginative personification of the giant buildings and the jungle-animal cars. This is an excellent example of the way writers animate inanimate objects in
order to allow us to see those objects as they appear
to someone else.

Moving to a new place, a new home, can often be a wrenching experience for a child. In the next poem, we see a little girl who looks upon a white rose as a new friend in a strange new place, only to lose even that small anchor and find herself totally alone. The poem is by a Micronesian student from a tiny island, Nukuoro.

A Little Girl with Her Second New Home

Her room had only one window
to the East
that she could look through,
and see a white rose.
It was blooming
every evening;
she could smell it
through the window.
As time swings by,
and things change,
She looks out
through the window,
seeing somebody taking away
the white rose,
and she is left alone
with nothing
but the voice
of her past memory.

— Iemima, age 19

Here is an expression of loneliness for someone
who is far away. Nighttime makes the loneliness grow.

. . . Soulfulness
is in me
as I harmonize the spell
of your name
under the shadow of evening stars —
for they form some distance
between us,
and my soul
always bears evening shadow's
burden.
— Osiaol, age 17

Since shadows are usually without substance or weight,
the phrase "bears evening shadow's burden" is a powerful one.

Older people often have to deal with loneliness.
We have seen several poems about old age in other
chapters, particularly in "People and More People," but
here is a short, evocative poem written in the voice of
the old person.

99
. . . Wrinkled face
and shaking muscles
engraved my body
for eternity.
Walking along my narrow path
I am entering
my 100's.
— Fabyan, age 20

Look at all the old words: *wrinkled, shaking, engraved,
eternity.* Why might a high school student see an old
person as "walking along my narrow path"?

This next poem was written in a summer workshop. The teacher has kindly allowed me to use it here. I am not sure of Russell's exact age.

Me in My Younger Years

A young man walked up to a roadside stand.
"Whacha sellin'?"
"Lemonade."
"How much?"
"Two cents a glass."
"Gimme a sample. Maybe I'll buy."
That was me in my younger years.
Now I have a weak heart and live
alone.

— Russell, upper elementary age

Think about ways to use fear as a subject for writing. What makes us afraid? Writers and tellers of ghost stories know. They tell of darkness, of running from a nameless horror, of beings from other planets, of other times. Nightmares are made of the wildest terrors our sleeping minds can show us. We fall. We peer over the edge of pits. We see snakes, wild animals; jaws await us, floors give way, we see ghoulish faces coming toward us.

Use the whole chalkboard for lists of fearful images, themes, and expressions. What animals are most fearful? How do they move? What do they find? How do they grab? Look at these words. What do they suggest to you?

tear	slash	scrape	slime
sneer	twist	claw	ooze
saliva	crush	slink	murky
creep	squeeze	slither	howl
silently	coil	glare	blood

Keep going — there are lots more words that we can

use for scaring ourselves! Two third graders wrote these poems about fear.

The Martians!
The Martians eat people!
They eat flesh of any kind.
Then they take a knife —
and then they give your bones
to the buzzards.

— Richard, age 9

A little girl was sitting in her
house and all of a sudden. . .
THE HOUSE CAVED IN!

— John, age 9

Micronesian folk tales abound with ghosts, like the ones which are terrifying the man in this next piece.

He's like a child in the forest,
surrounded by thick trees,
looking all around with blind eyes,
nothing in sight.
Soon darkness comes.
The rotten branches break
one by one.
The ghosts scratch his back.
He cries for help
but no one is beside him.
Screaming like shouting,
Shouting like screaming —
But, hands with no bones,
he's helpless
like an ant.

— Osiaol, age 17

224 *A Celebration of Bees*

Look at the effectiveness of the phrases, "looking all around with blind eyes," and "hands with no bones." They give us the sense of the poor man's feelings of terror and of utter helplessness.

Nightmares make wonderfully frightening subjects for writing, but only if you and your students remember to use the most powerful, carefully chosen words for your descriptions.

I'm falling and hanging to a vine in a deep, dark hole at the very middle, so that my intestine almost gets out of my mouth. As I look down, I see an image of a snake with open, waiting mouth. When I look up, a panther is there, waiting.

What shall I do with a fear of death . . . to be killed in a snake's mouth or a panther? Staying there, out of spirit, stumbling, I yell and yell — unconscious.

When I look again, panther is still there, but two white and black rats are taking turns to bite the vine. As my heart starts to beat faster and faster, it seems to me there isn't enough oxygen to breathe.

As the vine is cut, I fall like a whistling jet plane toward the bottom, heading for death. As the fear covers me, I yell and yell automatically, waking up with fear, trembling. Nightmare.

— Ulai, age 17

That was a nightmare. Two things work to make this piece a real and frightening experience. First, the writer has written in the present tense. We are plunged into a nightmare in progress. Second, the writer uses powerful descriptive comparisons to tell us what is happening in the nightmare: ". . . so that my intestine almost gets out of

my mouth. . . . . I fall like a whistling jet plane toward
the bottom . . . ."
    Let's look at a nightmare from northern Minnesota.

It vibrated, pounded,
    beated and throbbed.
I squatted, stooped,
    ducked and bobbed.
It howled, screamed,
    smirked and sneered.
I shrieked, sobbed,
    whined, and feared.
If they were near, I cried . . .
If they were here, I died.
    — Cay, high school

Cay uses rhyme that works here to form a chant of fear.
All of those active chase and evasion verbs with their
-ed endings mesmerize the reader into the fear that the
nightmare evokes.
    The ghoulish creature in this next picture has all of
the fearsome attributes that people everywhere give to
demons.

She wears her mask
of devil dead:
a long, crooked tongue,
gums made of gray jelly
and a single iron tooth.
Most of all,
she cries
with tears of blood.
In tomb
and dark cave
she always lives.
    — Sulikau, high school

Young poets, exploring "life" sometimes try to tackle the whole immense theme at once. A creative writing teacher once said to high school students, "Please. Don't begin your poem with 'Life is . . . .' " The two poems included here seem to have solved the "big bite" problem quite well. Each poet narrowed the topic.

Sometimes I Feel Like Crying

Sometimes, I feel like crying,
When I see a blind old man
guiding his white cane
in front of him.
But my friends would laugh.
Sometimes, I feel like crying,
When I hear a song
about war
or love.
But my friends would laugh.

Sometimes, I feel like crying,
When someone is unkind
to another.
But my friends would laugh.

I wonder if my friends
feel like crying
at these things too . . .
but I don't think so.

There must be
something
wrong with me.

— Pat, high school

Barb sees her journey through life as a trip through

a Mardi Gras, an arcade complete with colored lights, whirling balloons, and a hall of mirrors.

Living

We are involved in an arcade,
And we twirl and twist
Through its bewildering palisades of gaiety,
Confused and amazed by its brightness, and —
We are a Mardi Gras of decoration
As we wend the passages of blurred
Brilliance.

We are elated by the swirling
Redyelloworangeyellowred,
As we spring from ball to ball,
Our eyes fogged with cheer.

And then it is midnight —
In a hall of arched and smiling mirrors,
Our masques are unveiled.
What an unbelievable genesis is exhibited!
We have been masqued with ignorance.

But it is too late —
The arcade's doors have slammed,
Barred behind us.
The Mardi Gras has ended.

— Barb, high school

Death is another "big bite" theme; and unless one can pare it down to size, writing about death can be ponderous, bulky, even boring in spite of death's impact as a reality. A mind-stretching session, with words upon the board, is helpful. It becomes possible, then, to explore language for its cutting edge. And students will

find it easier to avoid huge generalities in favor of a
specific, crystallized moment or idea or image.

Death

Sad man lives today
people happy him —
    to no avail:
      death touched.
Flowers bloom his smile now —
    only until tomorrow.

— Nancy, high school

The anonymous poem below uses words and their
placement on the page for an effect. Using wide spacings
between some of the words encourages the reader to
pause slightly (try reading it aloud) and then a word like
glassful-smudge seems to rush out at once; *s m a s h e d*

has spaces between letters, and the word is slowed down
— like a slow-motion film of the act of smashing.

sans vie

the

　　　　lamp

lipped

its

　　　　　　　　　light

over the

　　　　　　　glassful-smudge

til

i

　　s m a s h e d

　　　　　　　　　it

with my

fist-

　　　　　　ful

　　　　　　of

　　　　　　darkness . . .
　　　　　— Anonymous

Living on relatively small and isolated islands,
usually in extended family situations, caused the Micronesian students to have a familiarity with death that
young people in our own culture experience less often.
　In his poem, Arthur captures the slowed action,

the dulled responses, the weighted feeling one has when
someone has died.

Death

Ding . . . ding . . . ding . . .
The bell rang slowly.
Each time the bell rang
it would last
for a long while.
The windless,
endless
horizon died out
and left
a tiny space
of the universe
to pass the dead sound
of the bell
to the alertless ears.

— Arthur, high school

Look at the words one at a time. They seem to have been
chosen for their stillness, their heaviness, even for the
sound of their slow-going vowels. Try to read this poem
in a bright, quick manner. It will resist you. Its language
forces you into a deliberate, quiet, sad reading.

A poem which has compared grieving people with
passengers on a ship who have lost their captain ends
with this moving image.

. . . as the earth
comes running over
the grave
and the dark night
falls
with no moon
nor star.

— Iemima, age 19

231   *Our Inner Spaces: Moods and Emotions*

We associate darkness, absence of color, with the idea of death.

> The gray clouds
> come toward me . . .
> the sky
> is now painted
> black,
> and the body
> is in the unexpected
> home —
> and sleep is forever.
>
> — Osiaol, age 17

Use of Color

Moods and emotions can be expressed in endless ways. One more tool can be added to the list: color. Most of us have our own characteristic reactions to color. We choose to live with certain colors in our homes; we dress in our favorite color; we often associate a color with a state of mind, a mood, or certain kinds of objects or people.

Earlier, we noticed a poem about death that used gray and black to underscore its bleakness. Here is a poem called "Black." What is its tone?

Black

Black is the life in the smouldering fire,
a tarnished old spoon,
the tongue of a liar.

Black's flat or sharp if you play the piano,
notes on a staff for the shrill-voiced soprano.

Black are the buttons on high-buttoned boots,
the coal in the coal-bin
the wrinkles in suits.

Black is a pencil point,
letters in print.
White where I washed the floor,
Black where I d'int.

Black is the face of a young Angus calf,
A poorly told joke
and a sarcastic laugh.
A raven, a panther, an inky toucan,
the rifle's report,
and the heart of the man
that refuses to pardon the faults
of all others
but expects to be treated by all
as a brother,
are as black as Death on her midnight prowl,
a voice in the night,
A hoot of an owl.

— Peter, age 14

Have you ever imagined colors that you can hear, smell, taste? Try it.

Gray
a musty smell
a dusty haste
a muffled sound
an aftertaste.

— Mary, high school

Think about lavender. What do you see? Is it a heavy color? Light? Can you touch it? What fabrics, textures do you feel? Does it have a shape? Shapes? How does it move?

Lavender

Lavender is a floating feeling;
Heavy and warm in a dream,
Gauzy and light on a cloud,
Rustling and free in the wind.

It is the song of a sparrow on a rainy day,
The empty silentude of an evening walk.
Lavender closes in when you're sad,
And rushes away in your happiness.

— Meri, high school

Lavender, violet, orchid, deepest purple. Think of these, and then read Carolyn's reactions.

Purple Thoughts

Torn by the breeze, violet streams through the air until it rests on the first lilacs. Their lavender scent lures the hummingbird and the little boy.

Waking violets are found in May baskets. Plums are found on the tree, and disappear when people walk by.

Purple is in the crayonpicture given to mother. And purple rings out its freedom song on liberty documents.

Tyrian purple rides to battle with the sovereign. And orchid dances, caught for a moment in the precious flower.

Then — purple velvet drapes my world.

— Carolyn, high school

Eight-year-old Kevin saw mountains when he thought about purple.

Purple mountains.
The sun makes the mountains
turn purple
and the mountains blue.
And purple moves slow
on the mountains.

— Kevin, age 8

Notice that Kevin visualizes a kind of heaviness when he sees purple. It "moves slow," he tells us. Do you see your special color moving?

This color moves in a particular way, too, according to Carolyn, and it has sound.

Green
Green grass,
Green flowers,
Green turtles,
Green weeds,
Green makes songs
from flowers, leaves.
It moves like snakes —
Silently.

— Carolyn L., age 8

Green also moves in this next poem, but it is not snakelike at all. How do you think green moves?

Green is grass,
trees,
and a cat's eyes.
It's dashing all over the world.
It tastes
like green grapes.

— Becky, age 8

Think about warm colors. Think about yellow:
What is yellow? What else? How does it taste? Has it
a fragrance? Emily Dickinson, in the poem that starts
"Ample make this bed . . .," spoke of the sunrise as
making a "yellow noise." Can you imagine it?

Orange. Surely you can smell this citrus perfume,
see its glow, taste its tartness. What else is orange? An
animal? A bird? An insect? Try a poem exercise that
places something vibrantly orange or red with something
cool and misty, like blue or lavender.

Can you see blue? Is it a mood? The blues are sad
songs about lost loves. Is blue a sad color for you?
Does the mention of blue set a particular scene in motion
for you? Perhaps you always think of blue in connection
with another color. Blue/green? Blue/white? Blue/black?
Blue/silver? What *is* blue?

Blue

Blue is a twilight time
when shadows
are among us
and the lazy people
stop sun-bathing
under
the cloudy blue sky.

— Pattie, age 10

Do you agree?

Most people can tell you about color — especially
their own favorites. In the classroom, try listing all the
likely and unlikely things a certain color suggests. List
moods and emotions; list birds, animals, forces of nature,
fabrics, sounds, tastes, fragrances, plants, jewels, insects,
musical instruments. If we jumble them all together,
what will we find? A skyful of violets? A trumpetsound
of lilies? Ruby raindrops? Feather-smoke gray moods?

"Our Inner Spaces" we called this chapter. They
are a labyrinth to explore. If you help your students
to find their way inside themselves, your reward will
certainly be as great as theirs.

Bibliography

Dickinson, Emily. "The bustle in a house." In *Selected Poems and Letters of Emily Dickinson*, edited by Robert Linscott. Garden City, N. Y.: Doubleday & Company, Inc., Anchor Books, 1959.

Esbensen, Barbara J. "Yellow." In *Swing Around the Sun*. Minneapolis, Minn.: Lerner Publications Co., 1965.

Frost, Robert. "Bereft," "Desert Places." In *Modern American Poetry*, edited by Louis Untermeyer. rev. ed. New York: Harcourt Brace Jovanovich, Inc., 1962.

Lewis, Richard, ed. "Feelings." In *Miracles: Poems by Children of the English-Speaking World*, pp. 151-182. New York: Simon and Schuster, Inc., 1966.

Millay, Edna St. Vincent. "Afternoon on a Hill." In *This Singing World: Junior Edition*, edited by Louis Untermeyer. New York: Harcourt Brace Jovanovich, Inc., 1926.

O'Neill, Mary. *Hailstones and Halibut Bones*. Garden City, N.Y.: Doubleday & Company, Inc., 1961.

Pratt, Agnes. "I'm Only Going To Tell You Once," "Death Takes Only a Minute." In *The Whispering Wind: Poetry by Young American Indians*, edited by Terry Allen. Garden City, N.Y.: Doubleday & Company, Inc., 1972.

Sandburg, Carl. "Cool Tombs." In *Modern American Poetry*, edited by Louis Untermeyer. rev. ed. New York: Harcourt Brace Jovanovich, Inc., 1962.

Wallace, Robert. "Moving." In *Some Haystacks Don't Even Have Any Needle: And Other Complete Modern Poems*, edited by Stephen Dunning, Edward Lueders, Hugh Smith. Glenview, Ill.: Scott, Foresman and Company, 1969.

Wright, James. "A Blessing." In *Some Haystacks Don't Even Have Any Needle: And Other Complete Modern Poems*, edited by Stephen Dunning, Edward Lueders, Hugh Smith. Glenview, Ill.: Scott, Foresman and Company, 1969.

SPARKLE, HOLLY, MERRY,
GOLDEN, TWINKLE, GLEAMING
CRIMSON, STREAMING,
GLOWING,
    WATCHFUL,
STARRY,
    WAITING,
HURRY,
    SUPPER,
    PRESENTS,
    WRAPPING,
JOY, GAY, HAPPY,
    BOUNCY, CRACK,
SMASH, TINKLE, BROKEN,
    SHOCK, QUIET,
    ANGER, MAD,
TIRED, SLEEPY,
    DROWSY. BED,
    WARM,
        SNUG,
            PEASE.

I LOVE YOU

Now Let's Write About . . .

In the haiku chapter we saw a film, *Goodnight Socrates*, used to motivate students to write. In that particular example, the film was used as a starting place for writing haiku. In these pages, I'd like to mention film and other media, both print and nonprint, as possibilities for motivating your students to write. I'd also like to give some more ideas about using mystery slips and other motivating techniques.

In spite of the fact that many, though I hope not most, audiovisual centers label their films as suitable for certain age groups, it has been my experience that most good films can be viewed by students of any age. Consider *The Red Balloon*,* which has been used with young children who focus on the magical balloon and the little boy's flight, finally, over the Paris rooftops, borne aloft by all the balloons in the city. But it has also been used in humanities classes in high school, where the sixteen to eighteen year olds look at it to find, beneath the magical balloon story, deeper meanings and searching questions about value systems and the human community. It would be a pity, as you will agree, to deny this richly rewarding motion picture to youngsters because someone has decided it is "too deep" — or to teenagers because someone else thinks it is "too babyish."

Another film which tells a story that can be seen on many levels is *The Golden Fish*. It involves a boy, a carnival wheel-of-chance, and the goldfish that the boy wins through a lucky spin of the wheel. It also has a wonderfully ominous man, dressed in black, an equally ominous black cat, and a caged bird.

*Distributors of all films mentioned here are listed in the Bibliography.

This poem is one young poet's response to the film.

Golden Fish

The bird
    Flew about his cage — knowing.
The fish
    Leapt through the air;
    To end floundering
    Upon the table top,
    Gasping for breath — knowing.
The boy
    Bespeckled and moptopped,
    A small muscular body
    Tanned as if it had never
    Met a winter's sun.
    Pin-wheels and hearts
    Caused his joy,
    His senses unaware as he entered.
The cat
    Sable coated, leapt from his
    Window of entrance; his
    Mouth tasted of fish and on
    His jet face
    Small drops of water.
    Images of pale feathers
    Tickled his dreams
    As he napped.

                  — Ann, age 17

Look at that last stanza, and compare it with the results
you might get from a more typical assignment to write
a report or review of the film, *The Golden Fish*. The very
fact of poetry forces a concentration on essentials that an

all-encompassing "theme" assignment never does for most students.

Another young poet, describing the same cat, writes:

. . . his black sheen
is taut
against his tense muscles.
He is alert
and ready to spring.
. . . But he is barred
from the bird
and cannot strike.
His glassy green eyes
cannot be pulled away
from
the flittering canary.

— Mary, age 17

Because there is almost no end to excellent films these days, there is almost no end to a list of them for writing purposes. Let me suggest a handful for your consideration. If your AV center does not own them, they can often be rented or obtained for preview with the idea of considering them for purchase at a later date. Many city and regional libraries own films that can be borrowed like books, along with the projector and screen. Other films, not locally available, can usually be found for you through an inter-library loan arrangement.

I have found that science films offer boundless opportunities for new approaches to writing. The Encyclopaedia Britannica films in the Basic Life Science series are excellent. Although usually classified junior high school or high school, these nature films are invaluable for use with younger children. I'm thinking especially of a film like *World in a Marsh*, a stunning twenty minutes or so that shows life above and below the surface of a marshland.

Neither you nor your young writers will ever again be able to look dispassionately at a dragonfly after seeing the activities of a dragonfly nymph at close range. One young viewer remarked, wide-eyed, "So *that's* why they're called dragonflies!" Take a look at the whole Basic Life Science series. It will be a rewarding task, I promise you.

The Sea is another excellent science film that can be used in many ways to encourage writing. It has gorgeous color, constant and varied movement of plants, animals, and water, and the incredible goings-on of an undersea environment.

Dream of the Wild Horses is a remarkable, short, color film showing a herd of horses in slow motion. The horses race along the seashore, through a wall of fire, wheeling and blazing, finally to soar, one by one, off rocky cliffs into the ocean below. No one, young or old, can resist the force and absolute beauty of this exotic film. Try to find it. You will be as enchanted by it as your students.

Still photographs can also be highly motivating. Most magazines today include a wealth of good photographs of people, animals, buildings, scenes from all over the world. Each one can be a spark-setter to the young writer's imagination.

Think about the kinds of questions that can be asked about each picture. What is the time of day? The weather? The mood of nature? The mood of the people or animals? Who is the picture about? What does it say to us? Can you become a part of the picture and tell about your own feelings? Answers to questions like these will start the writers on their way.

Use reproductions of paintings, too. Or take a trip to a local gallery and write ideas there on the spot, polishing them later in the classroom. (You will remember that this technique was also suggested in "People and More

People.'') After studying the Winslow Homer painting, *Gulf Stream*, Joseph wrote:

> In a boat among wind-tossed waves, I look and wonder what will happen to me. With sharks to the left and a gale to the right, I'm doomed. I can hear God calling me. But still I have to fight for my way of life and live.
>
> — Joseph, age 13

The work of Chagall has a childlike quality that children can easily respond to. The unreal scenes, with floating towns and people and animals seemingly happy to wander about upside down in an almost transparent world, appeal to their young imaginations. The painting *Dreams* inspired Tina.

Dreams

> Dreaming of things that are out of this world. Never knowing what colors or words they are saying. Seeing through things that aren't real. Houses upside-down and right-side-up. Hardly seeing anything but scary and funny people, jewels, houses, dresses, and millions of things that aren't real!
>
> — Tina, age 12

Tina also liked John Stuart Curry's painting, *Line Storm* and wrote:

> When the silence broke, everyone knew there was a storm brewing. They hurried and ran to get in but it wasn't easy. Everyone made it. Then it happened. The rain poured. A few minutes later, gone just as fast as it came!
>
> — Tina, age 12

It must be obvious, by now, that under your guid-
ance, almost anything can serve to stimulate your students
to write, no matter how old they are, or from what kinds
of backgrounds they've come to you.

Whether you use materials from the past or from
the present, the possibilities are there.

In earlier chapters, we have talked about the use of
mystery slips which are drawn from a box or jar and
contain an idea or subject to write about. As a variation
on this, try having two collections of slips on two different
colors of paper. Slips in the first color will have singular
or plural nouns written on them. Slips in the second color
may have verb forms or adjectives — the more unusual
the better, of course.

The following poems were all written in one session
of about an hour. Slips of colored paper were placed in
two big glass bowls. The slips were folded in half to make
them more secret and special. As each child picked *one
from each bowl*, there was much groaning and forehead
smacking, since these combinations struck the children as
impossibilities. So, we decided that each dissatisfied
customer could exchange *one* slip for a different one of
the same color. Some did. Others decided not to risk an
even greater impossibility. And the writing began.

Our rule was that the two words *must* be used *together*. That is, no other word could come between them.
It did not matter in what order the words were used.

These poems were the result of this motivating
technique.

Windy
rooftops blowing.
Sky is thin.
Wicked clouds
run away
howling.

— Kathy McD., age 13

Cars rushing in all directions
Odd feelings come to me
When near the *foggy streets.*
Shadows lurking everywhere.
I draw nearer to my father,
Clutching his hand
furiously.

— Wendy H., age 11

Listen!
The wind's howling.
Look!
The grass is swaying.
See the *treetops' shimmering* leaves:
Autumn.

— Emily M., age 10

Strawberry windows
with sun
shining in.
Super-fresh fruit
picked out of a garden.
The sun sets
over the farm.
It rains on many of days
in the spring.
Strawberry windows.

— Mary M., age 9

Misty doorways
like boxes of fog
with a board cutting the cloud
in half.
When the board moves,
misty doorways
are open.

— Emily M., age 10

Lemon daisies
and
strawberry grasses
blend
with the plum shadows
of trees
to make a fresh, flowery
field of sweetness.

— Mary Anne C., age 16

This particular idea starter proved to be one of the all-time favorites in classrooms. The students spent their extra time dipping into the bowls for the two slips of colored paper that gave them, it seems, such a good push into the world of imaginative writing.

Look again at Emily's poem beginning, "Misty doorways." It is impossible to imagine that, *without those particular two slips of paper,* Emily would have come up with anything remotely resembling this word picture. Under what other circumstances would Emily have pictured those "doorways like boxes of fog"? Boxes of fog! Have you ever spoken or written or thought about boxes of fog? Neither had Emily, of course. But once she began to see those misty doorways, they became real for her. The shape of doorways, the texture of mist, and synonyms for the word *misty* are worked together to help her to expand her imaginative vision. Only then could she tell us of this vision and let us see the solid door as "a board cutting the cloud in half."

Another way to use the simple, subject matter starter slip is to suggest that the subject itself never be actually mentioned in the poem or in the title. The idea for the riddle poem came from a session in which we read May Swenson's marvelous books of poetry, *Poems to Solve* and *More Poems to Solve*. (See the Bibliography at the end of this book.)

With an absolutely bewitching use of words, May Swenson gives us familiar objects, animals, plants, woodland scenes, and tells all *by speaking about other things*. In her poems, the answer is rarely given. Sometimes she does help us by putting it in tiny print at the bottom of the page.

One group of children printed the answers to their riddle poems upside down in the bottom corner of their paper. Try not to look at the answers to the following poems until you have really tackled the poem.

1. Swiftly
   on bent wire legs
   he moves without a sound
   going down a thin ladder
   for food.

   — Mary M., age 9

2. Prowling.
   Fierce daisy faces,
   staring with topaz eyes
   paws moving in the leaves.
   Sneaking.

   — Emily M., age 10

3. Growling at the moonlight,
   looking for a fight.
   Sharp points stab,
   rumbling sounds roam in the dark.

   — Wendy H., age 11

4. Creeping
   garden hose
   with plaid back.
   A lightning-quick forked path
   Searches the air.
   — Mary Anne, age 16

5. Reaching
   twisted, crooked
   up toward the sky above.
   Arms pointing down to the dirt floor.
   Lovely.
   — Kathy McD., age 13

6. Spikes hitting leaves —
   a wall of stalagtites —
   the noise is like tearing a sheet —
   enormous monster.
   — Caroline L., age 10

7. Like scissors
   cut paper,
   it is pulled or it pulls.
   It makes a rumbling noise
   in the afternoon.
   — Pattie Van D., age 10

8. Prison
   locking in teeth.
   Teeth wait for warden
   to come to take off the bars.
   — Sue Van D., age 12

1. spider   2. lions   3. thunder   4. snake   5. branches
6. rake   7. lawnmower   8. braces

Since the rule is that the subject can never be mentioned by name, you can see how each writer has been forced to see that subject in terms of something else. It is an exercise that is challenging to writer and reader alike.

Some Random Suggestions

See *This Fabulous Century* series (Time-Life Books, 1969) for superb photographs of life in America, 1900-1960.

Peer through a magnifying glass at familiar objects and describe them in new ways.

See pond water through a microscope.

Using a microscope (or a microprojector) look at pollen, cells, insect legs, leaf structure, grains of various chemicals.

Using mirrors, see the mirror-image world Alice saw. Step into it and write!

Bring a variety of objects to class, each object having a definite odor or fragrance and describe each.

Take a flower apart and describe each part in new and imaginative terms. See comparisons you never thought of before.

Watch someone blow up a balloon. Describe it at every stage as it is filling with air. (Perhaps the *opposite* is occurring in the blower?)

Look at the sidewalk or street with a magnifying glass. Describe what is revealed. Insects? Particles of stone, glass, tar? Compare the cracks with something else.

Pick out a stranger and try to *see into* that person's real self. Look for clues. What do hands tell you? Eyes? Shoes?

Overhear a conversation between strangers. Write one sentence of it as part of a piece of poetry. What else can you add? What conclusions can you draw from what you overheard?

Try using sound as a motivator. Recordings of music, voices, pure sound — all can be valuable to the writer. Sound tapes of all kinds are available, and students can make their own, too, and offer them for the other students' creative efforts.

Find recordings of electronic music and try these.

The sound is often so unfamiliar that the listener must use the mind and *see* the sounds.

Let players of particular instruments play a simple scale. It is a challenge to a writer to find words to depict the sounds made by, for instance, a flute, and to find words to describe the same scale as played by a bassoon, or a harp.

The Paul Torrence album, "Sounds and Images" (Ginn & Co.) is an excellent way to begin working with sounds, since it is specifically written to release creative expression in the listener. And any record library offers musical works from every age that are good for this kind of imagining. Play Villa-Lobos' *Little Train of the Caipira,* without telling the students the title and see what kind of images you get from them. Play Debussy, Ravel, Prokofiev, Stravinsky, Chopin — try anything and everything.

That has been the theme of this book, has it not? I hope you have shaken off all doubts and fears and anxieties about what is the right thing to write about. Anything goes. You never know what simple suggestion from you will be the flint to strike a creative spark in a young mind that doesn't yet know it will soon be ablaze with undreamed-of imaginative powers.

I wish you well.

Bibliography

From the great numbers and kinds of films, recordings, and art works available, I've listed only a relatively small sampling. I've found these to be effective in my work with young writers, but there are hundreds more, I'm sure. Remember: virtually *anything* can stimulate one's imagination.

I hope you will use the following lists as a jumping-off place for further exploration of all media.

Films

Basic Life Science Series. Chicago: Encyclopaedia Britannica Educational Corporation. (All films in this series should be considered as good possibilities.)

Dream of the Wild Horses. 9 minutes, color. New York: Contemporary Films/McGraw-Hill. (A stunning, evocative slow-motion study of horses as they rush through flames, across the land, and sail off a cliff into the sea. Effective uses in creative writing and as an impetus for painting as well.)

Eugene Atget. 10 minutes, b/w. New York: Contemporary Films/McGraw-Hill.

Elsa and Her Cubs. 31 minutes, color. Briarcliff Manor, N.Y.: Benchmark Films.

Eskimo in Life and Legend, The. 22 minutes, color & b/w. Chicago: Encyclopaedia Britannica Educational Corporation.

Eskimo Summer. 16 minutes, color. Chicago: International Film Bureau, Inc.

Golden Fish, The. 20 minutes, color. New York: Columbia University Press.

Goodnight Socrates. 34 minutes, b/w. New York: Contemporary Films/McGraw-Hill.

Great Adventure. 80 minutes, b/w. New York: Sterling Educational Films. (This film can be shown with a short "intermission," if necessary.)

Haiku. 29 minutes. New York: Columbia University Press. (Uses literal and abstract photography to capture the essence of haiku.)

Life of a Dragonfly, The. 10 minutes, color & b/w. Los
   Angeles: Baily Film Associates.
Monarch Butterfly Story, The. 2nd edition. 11 minutes,
   color. Chicago: Encyclopaedia Britannica Education-
   al Corporation.
Nahanni. 19 minutes, color. New York: Contemporary
   Films/McGraw-Hill.
Red Balloon, The. 34 minutes, color. New York: CCM
   Films, Inc.
Sea, The. 26 minutes, color. Chicago: Encyclopaedia
   Britannica Educational Corporation.
Sea Sorcery. 15 minutes, color. New York: Contemporary
   Films/McGraw-Hill.
Smile, The (Le Sourire). 18 minutes, color. New York:
   Contemporary Films/McGraw-Hill.
String Bean. 17 minutes, color & b/w in the same film.
   New York: Contemporary Films/McGraw-Hill.
Synchromy. 8 minutes, color. New York: Learning Cor-
   poration of America.
Talking Hands. 20 minutes, color. Norman, Okla.: Univer-
   sity of Oklahoma Press.
Time Piece. 8 minutes, color. Van Nuys, Calif.: Creative
   Film Society. (An unusual film, imaginatively
   showing the urban "rat-race.")
Universe. 26 minutes, b/w. New York: McGraw-Hill Films.
Very Nice, Very Nice. 7 minutes, b/w. New York: Con-
   temporary Films/McGraw-Hill. (An experimental
   film showing contemporary society in an era of
   brinkmanship.)
World in a Marsh. 25 minutes, color. New York: McGraw-
   Hill Films.

Recordings
Copeland, Aaron. *Quiet City for Trumpet, English Horn,
   Orch.* (1940).
_____. *Red Pony.*
Delius, Frederick. *Brigg Fair, English Rhapsody* (1908).
_____. *Sleigh Ride.*

Ibert, Jacques. *Divertissement* (1930).

Prokofiev, Serge. *Lieutenant Kijé Suite, Op. 60* (1934).

_____. *Scythian Suite, Op. 20.*

Saint-Saëns, Camille. *Carnival of the Animals.*

_____. *Danse macabre, Op. 40.*

Satie, Erik. *Trois Gymnopédies* (1888).

Villa-Lobos, Heitor. *Little Train of the Caipira.*

Art

(Sources for art reproductions.)

Artext Prints, Incorporated
Westport, CT   06880
    (8" x 10" size available. Catalogues.)

Associated American Artists
711 Fifth Avenue
New York, NY 10036

Braun Prints
Graphic Arts Unlimited
225 Fifth Avenue
New York, NY   10010
    (8" x 10" pictures are $1.00 each.)

Museum of Modern Art
11 West 53rd Street
New York, NY   10019

National Archives and Records Service, The
General Services Administration
Washington, DC   20408
    Select Picture List Negro Art from the Harmon Collection.
    (Black and white prints only. 8" x 10" are $2.00 each.
    These are photographic copies of the original works
    of art.)

New York Graphic Society, Ltd.
Greenwich, CT   06830

Oestreicher's Prints, Inc.
43 West 46th Street
New York, NY   10036

Penn Prints
572 Fifth Avenue
New York, NY   10036

In addition, see this book, available at most libraries: *A Guide to Color Reproductions* by Margaret Bartan, 2nd edition, Scarecrow Press, Inc., Metuchen, New Jersey, 1971.

Paintings

Cafe scenes by Henri Toulouse-Lautrec.

Almost anything by Honore Daumier.

The *Disasters of War* series by Fransisco Goya.

Bruegel, Pieter, the Elder. *Winter: Hunters in the Snow.*
de la Tour, Georges. *The Fortune Teller.*
Hofer, Karl. *Three Masks.*
Homer, Winslow. *Gulf Stream.*
Klee, Paul. *Tomcat.*
Marc, Franz. *Blue Horses.*
Marsh, Reginald. *The Merry-go-round.*
Picasso, Pablo. *The Ironer.*
Roualt, Georges. *Sad Clown.*
Turner, J.M.W. *Snowstorm.*
Van Gogh, Vincent. *Church at Anvers.*
_____. *Starry Night.*
_____. *Potato Eaters.*
Wood, Grant. *American Gothic.*
Wyeth, Andrew. *Chambered Nautilus.*
_____. *Christina's World.*

A Selected Bibliography of Poems for Children

Adams, Adriene. *Poetry of Earth*. New York: Charles Scribner's Sons, 1972.

Adoff, Arnold, ed. *I Am the Darker Brother: An Anthology of Modern Poems by Black Americans*. New York: The Macmillan Company, 1970.

———. *Black Out Loud: An Anthology of Modern Poems by Black Americans*. New York: The Macmillan Company, 1970.

———. *City in All Directions*. New York: The Macmillan Company, 1969.

*Allen, Terry, ed. *The Whispering Wind: Poetry by Young American Indians*. Garden City, N.Y.: Doubleday & Company, Inc., 1972.

Arbuthnot, May H., and Root, S. L., Jr., compilers. *Time for Poetry*. rev. ed. Glenview, Ill.: Scott, Foresman and Company, 1968.

Atwood, Ann. *Haiku: The Mood of the Earth*. New York: Charles Scribner's Sons, 1971.

Bashō. *The Way of Silence: The Prose and Poetry of Bashō*. Edited by Richard Lewis. New York: Dial Press, Inc., 1970.

Behn, Harry, trans. *Cricket Songs: Japanese Haiku*. New York: Harcourt Brace Jovanovich, Inc., 1964.

———. *More Cricket Songs: Japanese Haiku*. New York: Harcourt Brace Jovanovich, Inc., 1971.

Behn, Harry. *Golden Hive*. New York: Harcourt Brace Jovanovich, Inc., 1966.

———. *Little Hill*. New York: Harcourt Brace Jovanovich, Inc., 1949.

Belting, Natalia. *Winter's Eve*. New York: Holt, Rinehart and Winston, Inc., 1969.

Bierhorst, John, ed. *In the Trail of the Wind: American Indian Poems and Ritual Orations*. New York: Farrar, Straus and Giroux, Inc., 1971.

*Poetry written by young writers.

Bogan, Louise, and Smith, William J., compilers. *Golden Journey: Poems for Young Children*. Chicago: Reilly and Lee Company, 1965.

Coatsworth, Elizabeth. *Sparrow Bush*. New York: Grosset and Dunlap, Inc., n.d.

Cole, William, ed. *Birds and the Beasts Were There*. New York: World Publishing Company, 1963.

Dickinson, Emily. *Selected Poems and Letters of Emily Dickinson*. Edited by Robert Linscott. Garden City, N.Y.: Doubleday & Company, Inc., Anchor Book, 1959.

Dunning, Stephen; Lueders, Edward; and Smith, Hugh; eds. *Reflections on a Gift of Watermelon Pickle and Other Modern Verse*. West Caldwell, N.J.: Lothrop, Lee and Shepard Company, 1967.

———. *Some Haystacks Don't Even Have Any Needle: And Other Complete Modern Poems*. West Caldwell, N.J.: Lothrop, Lee and Shepard Company, 1969.

Esbensen, Barbara J. *Swing Around the Sun*. Minneapolis, Minn.: Lerner Publications Company, 1965.

Frost, Robert. *In the Clearing*. New York: Holt, Rinehart and Winston, Inc., 1962.

———. *You Come Too*. New York: Holt, Rinehart and Winston, Inc., 1959.

Giovanni, Nikki. *Ego Tripping and Other Poems for Young Readers*. New York: Lawrence Hill and Company, 1974.

Hannum, Sara, and Chase, John T., eds. *The Wind Is Round*. New York: Atheneum Publishers, 1970.

Henderson, Harold G., ed. *An Introduction to Haiku, an Anthology of Poems and Poets from Basho and Shiki*. Garden City, N.Y.: Doubleday & Company, Inc., 1958.

Hoban, Russell. *The Pedaling Man and Other Poems*. New York: Grosset and Dunlap, Inc., 1968.

Holman, Felice. *At the Top of My Voice and Other Poems*. New York: Grosset and Dunlap, Inc., 1970.

_____. *I Hear You Smiling and Other Poems.* New York: Charles Scribner's Sons, 1973.

Hood, Flora M. *The Turquoise Horse: Prose and Poetry of the American Indian.* New York: G. P. Putnam's Sons, 1972.

Hopkins, Lee Bennett. *On Our Way: Poems of Pride and Love.* New York: Alfred A. Knopf, Inc., 1974.

Hopkins, Lee B., ed. *The City Spreads Its Wings.* New York: Franklin Watts, Inc., 1970.

*_____. *City Talk.* New York: Alfred A. Knopf, Inc., 1970.

Hubbell, Patricia. *Apple Vendor's Fair.* New York: Atheneum Publishers, 1963.

_____. *Catch Me a Wind.* New York: Atheneum Publishers, 1968.

_____. *Eight A.M. Shadows.* New York: Atheneum Publishers, 1965.

Hughes, Langston. *Don't You Turn Back.* Edited by Lee B. Hopkins. New York: Alfred A. Knopf, Inc., 1969. (Original title: *I Bring You My Songs: Poems by Langston Hughes.*)

_____. *Dream Keeper.* New York: Alfred A. Knopf, Inc., 1932.

Issa. *A Few Flies and I: Haiku by Issa.* Edited by Jean Merrill and Ronni Solbert. New York: Pantheon Books, Inc., 1969.

Jordan, June. *Who Look at Me.* New York: Thomas Y. Crowell Company, 1969.

*Jordan, June, and Bush, Terri, eds. *The Voice of the Children.* New York: Holt, Rinehart and Winston, Inc., 1970.

*Joseph, Stephen M. *The Me Nobody Knows: Children's Voices from the Ghetto.* New York: Avon Books, 1972.

Krauss, Ruth. *The Cantilever Rainbow.* New York: Pantheon Books, Inc., 1965.

*Larrick, Nancy, ed. *I Heard a Scream in the Street: Poems by Young People in the City.* New York: M. Evans and Company, Inc., 1970.

———. *On City Streets*. New York: M. Evans and Company, Inc., 1968.

———. *Piper, Pipe That Song Again*. New York: Random House, Inc., 1965.

Lewis, Richard. *Out of the Earth I Sing*. New York: Grosset and Dunlap, Inc., 1968.

Lewis, Richard, ed. *I Breathe a New Song: Poems of the Eskimo*. New York: Simon and Schuster, Inc., 1971.

*———. *Miracles: Poems by Children of the English-Speaking World*. New York: Simon and Schuster, Inc., 1966.

———. *Of This World: A Poet's Life in Poetry*. New York: Dial Press, Inc., 1968. (Author note: The Japanese poet Issa is one of the most famous Haiku poets.)

*———. *There Are Two Lives: Poems by Children of Japan*. New York: Simon and Schuster, Inc., 1970.

Livingston, Myra C. *The Malibu and Other Poems*. New York: Atheneum Publishers, Inc., 1972.

Merriam, Eve. *Finding a Poem*. New York: Atheneum Publishing, Inc., 1970.

———. *Out Loud*. New York: Atheneum Publishers, Inc., 1973.

Moore, Lilian. *I Thought I Heard the City*. New York: Atheneum Publishers, Inc., 1969.

O'Neill, Mary. *People I'd Like To Keep*. Garden City, N.Y.: Doubleday & Company, Inc., 1964.

———. *Take a Number*. Garden City, N.Y.: Doubleday & Company, Inc., 1968.

———. *Winds*. Garden City, N.Y.: Doubleday & Company, Inc., 1971.

———. *Words Words Words*. Garden City, N.Y.: Doubleday & Company, Inc., 1966.

Plotz, Helen, ed. *Imagination's Other Place: Poems of Science and Mathematics*. New York: Thomas Y. Crowell Company, 1955.

———. *Untune the Sky: Poems of Music and the Dance*. New York: Thomas Y. Crowell Company, 1957.

Rexroth, Kenneth, trans. *One Hundred Poems from the Japanese*. New York: New Directions Publishing Corp., 1955.

Sandburg, Carl. *Early Moon*. New York: Harcourt Brace Jovanovich, Inc., 1958.

_____. *Honey & Salt*. New York: Harcourt Brace Jovanovich, Inc., 1963.

_____. *Wind Song*. New York: Harcourt Brace Jovanovich, Inc., 1960.

Summerfield, Geoffrey, ed. *First Voices One*. New York: Alfred A. Knopf, Inc., 1971. (An anthology of poetry and pictures.)

_____. *First Voices Two*. New York: Alfred A. Knopf, Inc., 1971.

_____. *First Voices*. Vol. 3. New York: Alfred A. Knopf, Inc., 1972.

_____. *First Voices*. Vol. 4. New York: Alfred A. Knopf, Inc., 1972.

Swenson, May. *A Cage of Spines*. New York: Rinehart and Company, Inc., 1958.

_____. *More Poems to Solve*. New York: Charles Scribner's Sons, 1970.

_____. *Poems to Solve*. New York: Charles Scribner's Sons, 1970.

Teasdale, Sara. *Collected Poems of Sara Teasdale*. Edited by Marya Zaturenska. New York: The Macmillan Company, 1953.

_____. *Stars To-Night*. New York: The Macmillan Company, 1930.

Untermeyer, Louis, ed. *Modern American Poetry*. rev. ed. New York: Harcourt Brace Jovanovich, Inc., 1962.

*Volavkova, H., ed. *I Never Saw Another Butterfly*. New York: McGraw-Hill Book Company, 1964.

Recordings

Caedmon #TC1387. *Poems by a Little Girl*. Hilda Conkling. 1970.

Caedmon #TC1227. *Miracles*. Richard Lewis. 1967.

Ginn and Company. *Sounds and Images*. Paul Torrence.

Books for Adults

Applegate, Mauree. *Easy in English*. New York: Harper & Row, Publishers, 1960.

Arnstein, Flora J. *Children Write Poetry: A Creative Approach*. 2nd ed. New York: Dover Publications, 1967.

_____. *Poetry in the Elementary Classroom*. New York: Appleton Century Crofts, 1962.

Cole, Natalie R. *Arts in the Classroom*. New York: John Day Company, Inc., 1940.

_____. *Children's Arts from Deep Down Inside*. New York: John Day Company, Inc., 1966.

Hughes, Ted. *Poetry Is*. Garden City, N.Y.: Doubleday & Company, Inc., 1970. (Original title: *Poetry in the Making.)*

Koch, Kenneth. *Rose, Where Did You Get That Red?* New York: Random House, Inc., 1973.

_____. *Wishes, Lies, and Dreams: Teaching Children To Write Poetry*. New York: Random House, Inc., Vintage Trade Books, 1971.

Index of Poets' Ages

Note: You can use this index to find poems that were written by children from the age group you are working with.

Seven year olds wrote the poems found on the following pages:
129, 130, 151

Eight year olds wrote the poems found on the following pages:
36, 38, 42, 44, 80, 88, 100, 103, 106, 107, 108, 109, 112, 113, 114, 119, 137, 138, 143, 146, 148, 151, 152, 153, 157, 158, 163, 201, 207, 209, 214, 215, 216, 217, 235

Nine year olds wrote the poems found on the following pages:
16, 27, 28, 29, 30, 37, 38, 39, 102, 104, 107, 108, 109, 111, 112, 113, 121, 122, 129, 147, 152, 162, 215, 224, 245, 247

Ten year olds wrote the poems found on the following pages:
11, 15, 17, 36, 44, 53, 63, 67, 68, 81, 89, 91, 101, 102, 105, 106, 108, 110, 124, 125, 127, 128, 135, 136, 137, 144, 145, 147, 148, 149, 152, 155, 156, 157, 158, 161, 163, 173, 175, 176, 188, 190, 192, 198, 201, 206, 208, 209, 236, 245, 246, 247, 248

Eleven year olds wrote the poems found on the following pages:
51, 52, 53, 54, 56, 61, 81, 82, 86, 87, 89, 92, 95, 120, 125, 126, 135, 136, 139, 146, 147, 148, 149, 154, 164, 169, 172, 178, 185, 186, 187, 189, 206, 245, 247

Twelve year olds wrote the poems found on the following pages:
17, 27, 52, 54, 55, 63, 87, 110, 120, 121, 124, 125, 153, 154, 156, 170, 175, 205, 208, 209, 218, 223, 243, 248

Thirteen year olds wrote the poems found on the following pages:
56, 63, 64, 68, 69, 74, 118, 122, 127, 168, 173, 174, 177, 187, 188, 198, 199, 202, 206, 207, 210, 243, 244, 248

Fourteen year olds wrote the poems found on the following pages:
65, 67, 70, 71, 73, 75, 76, 96, 105, 138, 232

High school students wrote the poems found on the following pages:
40, 41, 69, 76, 84, 85, 88, 89, 90, 92, 93, 95, 104, 118, 123, 134, 135, 136, 139, 140, 141, 161, 165, 166, 167, 168, 169, 170, 171, 172, 184, 186, 187, 190, 191, 192, 193, 202, 203, 204, 205, 216, 217, 218, 219, 220, 221, 222, 224, 225, 226, 227, 228, 229, 231, 232, 233, 234, 240, 241, 246, 248

Acknowledgments

To thank individually all the young people whose poems fill this book would be impossible, for most of them are all grown up and scattered now to unknown places. They once met with me in classes in Eureka, California; Duluth and Minneapolis, Minnesota; Tallahassee, Florida; Taipei, Taiwan; and on the islands of Yap, Palua, Ponape, Truk, and the Marshall Islands in Micronesia.

There are others, however, whom I *can* thank, by naming them:

— Sister Joan Braun, director, and Mary Jane Kumsha, assistant director, Scholastica Library, Duluth, and the other gracious people there who provided me with a drawer, a table, and that blessed library serenity in which to write;

— Sister Margaret James Laughlin, former principal of Stanbrook Hall High School in Duluth, for permission to use art work done by my art students there, 1965-1967;

— Diane Boeser, who doggedly transcribed the often illegible rough draft from handwritten scrawl to publisher-reader manuscript;

— Jeanette Knabe, whose eagle eyes discovered the invisible errors and awkward phrasing that had escaped author and typist;

— my husband, Thorwald Esbensen, for his willingness to read and discuss every phase of this book, and for his encouragement (bordering on insistence) that I write it at all;

— our children, Julie, Daniel, Jane, and George, who not only allowed me to include some of their poems, but who put in some long, eight-hour days caring for the baby, Kai, so I could slip away to Scholastica a few days each week to write.

And I need to speak here of our son, Peter, whose interest in my creative work with children was unflagging and enthusiastic. This is the book he hoped I'd get around to writing. He died before he could see it and find in it the poem he contributed to Mother's collection.

About the Author

Barbara Juster Esbensen is a writer and poet who has worked with children in creative arts since 1945. She has taught creative writing to students of all ages, children to adults. Most recently she taught creative writing for teachers at the College of St. Scholastica in Duluth, Minnesota and conducted a private poetry studio for children and adolescents. Mrs. Esbensen is also a painter with a degree in Art Education from the University of Wisconsin.

Published work includes: *Swing Around the Sun*, a book of poetry for children, Lerner Publications, Minneapolis, 1965; poems in *Time for Poetry*, revised edition, compiled by May H. Arbuthnot and S. L. Root, Jr., Scott, Foresman and Company, 1968; *Cyclo-Teachers*, programmed series in language arts, World Book Inc., 1962; author of *Evaluative Instruments for National Reading Assessment Program*, Science Research Associates, 1964; poems published in *The Moccasin*, League of Minnesota Poets magazine.